THE ARCHITECT
RECONSTRUCTING HER PRACTICE

The MIT Press   Cambridge, Massachusetts   London, England

EDITED BY FRANCESCA HUGHES

THE ARCHITECT
RECONSTRUCTING HER PRACTICE

For Jonathan

This book was printed and bound in the United States of America.

Library of Congress Cataloging-in-Publication Data

The architect : reconstructing her practice / edited by Francesca Hughes.

    p.   cm.

    Includes bibliographical references and index.

    ISBN 0-262-08245-4 (hardcover : alk. paper)

    1. Women-owned architectural firms—Management.   2. Women architects—Psychology.   3. Gender identity.   4. Structuralism.   I. Hughes, Francesca.

NA1997.A68   1996

720'.82—dc20   96-3167

                                                          CIP

CONTENTS

ACKNOWLEDGMENTS

In the long slow labor that is this book I have been blessed by the generosity, wit, and patience of many. To all that have put up with it, and me, and the absences I have incurred in the rest of my life, I am deeply grateful.

This project would never have started nor survived without the unquestioning support of Iain Boyd Whyte at the Centre for Architectural History and Theory at Edinburgh University, who first suggested "some work be done" on the subject. He remained throughout the process steadfastly there; patient, critical, witty, and wise. I could not have asked for better guidance as he continued to nurture and tease this project into existence, well into its adulthood. The generosity implicit is rare. I am honored and touched.

I am, of course, indebted to all the authors, whom I would like to thank for their good humor, criticism, and patience and for never making it feel like a "debt."

I am also very grateful to the Architectural Association, and the then Chairman Alan Balfour, for inviting several of the papers to be given as a lecture series in what proved crucial in the crystallization of the ideas. To the General Studies staff there for their always excellent moderation and support and to Katherine Clark, Micki Hawkes, and Jane McGrath for their dedicated help.

I am also grateful to:

Nasrine Seraji for the gender changer and Oscar Stevenson and Sarah Allan for their work on it. Dennis Gilbert, Rainer Hofmann, and Norbert Miguletz, who generously contributed their photographs.

The many friends and colleagues with whom I have discussed the project and have been key in large and small ways to its development, to them all I am very grateful: Catherine Burd, Katie Lloyd Thomas, Natasha Nicholson, Bryan Potter, Katerina Ruedi, Ottelie Stevenson.

My family for their support and especially Robert and Jackie Meyer who, with typical grace, generously allowed this appendage to temporarily invade their lives.

Carolyn Gill at Birkbeck College for her warm words of encouragement and editorial advice.

I owe a special debt to Roger Conover at MIT Press for his timely intervention and to Jean Wilcox for her excellent work on the design.

I would also like to here publicly thank four people who, in ways that exceed what can be said, have made this and much more possible: Jennifer Bloomer, Bill Carswell, Tom Phillips, and my mother, Psiche Bertini Hughes. For opening me to the possibility of a more complex understanding of things. For their never pedagogical grace.

Lastly, there is a ghost-editor-dictionary-and-critic at work here, husband, partner, support-system, and muse, Jonathan Meyer. This is his labor too, and is for him.

An Introduction

Francesca Hughes

What if we were to approach . . . the area of a relationship to the other where the code of sexual marks would no longer be discriminating? The relationship would not be asexual, far from it, but would be sexual otherwise: beyond the binary difference that governs the decorum of all codes, beyond the opposition feminine/masculine, beyond bisexuality as well, beyond homosexuality and heterosexuality which come to the same thing. As I dream of saving the chance that this question offers, I would like to believe in the multiplicity of sexually marked voices. I would like to believe in the masses, this indeterminable number of blended voices, this mobile of non-identified sexual marks whose choreography can carry, divide, multiply the body of each "individual," whether he be classified as "man" or "woman" according to the criteria of usage.

—*Jacques Derrida*[1]

Derrida's reverie of voices that are marked sexually beyond the confines of the binary coupling, though hopelessly idealist, remains compelling. Perhaps more of a *cris de coeur* than a reverie, it speaks to a richness and fluidity of understanding that might render a once worn and exasperated argument about gender, identity, and sexual discrimination suddenly open to more promising possibilities that evade the rut in which so many of these conversations get stuck.

The absence of women from the profession of architecture remains, despite the various theories, very difficult to explain and very slow to change. It demarcates a failure the profession has become adept at turning a blind eye to, despite the fact that it places architecture far behind the other professions with which architects frequently seek to align themselves.[2] If we consider architecture a cultural construct, both vessel and residue, we can but wonder what this symptomatic absence suggests about our culture and the orders that govern the production of its architecture. One thing is clear however: just as the absence of either sex from a large constituency must indicate some internal crisis in which gender plays a crucial role, the absence of women from the profession points to a profound gender-related crisis at the base of architecture.

The troping of gender in architecture, through the figure of the feminine, is complex. Chameleonlike, the question of gender very quickly hides itself in the shifting territory of metaphor, reification, and the real that makes up architecture. The muse, the ideology, the icon-object that is vessel, and the law all provide safe houses for the furtive category of gender (and, by the same turn, sexuality). A tracing of this thread draws a convoluted line, full of loops and false knots, that become particularly entangled around the question of architectural *practice* and gender, always already made pointed by the metaphorical relations between architecture and gender that are the (undesirable) legacy of every architect.

The same tradition that binds the female body to the earth (both fertile vessels) genders other vessels and their making, binding the female to architecture. Architecture, a container in more ways than one, is also figured as female.[3]

So gender slips into the body of architecture, via the body of woman. But within this process a crucial turn allows the constitution of gender to shift from "female" to "feminine": architecture, like musical composition, painting, and poetry, is feminine. Where does all of this troping leave the female? Casting architecture as feminine renders its muse female and consequently induces a necessary crisis of identity for the female architecture maker: How is the architect to be seduced by the muse, to succumb to her grace, if she too is female?[4] The muse, being feminine, is endowed with all of the features that will make her the object of desire for men: voluptuous, half-clad, white, and unavailable. By inviting a relationship that must be sexual, that must be with men, in other words, she excludes the very image that she projects. Any relationship that the female architecture maker might construct with the muse must be oblique, slippery, and unstable.

However, on closer inspection, we find that though convoluted, the construction of this siting is consistent in its exclusive transferral of the feminine only to the female and the masculine only to the male: gender is, here, essentially discrete. This siting relies on a fixity of gender; remove this fixity, and it collapses. If gender is considered unstable, multiple for instance, exactly this will occur.[5]

The potential displacement of the excluding mechanisms of a (strategically) gendered discourse by the possibility of multiple gender is compelling: gender resisting fixity, without abandoning the figures of a gendered discourse. Multiple gender as an agent that provides the necessary slippage for any gender to inhabit any discourse.[6]

But inevitably, if we try to pursue this thread further, we return to the age-old problem of language and transparency: how to investigate the possibility of gender beyond the fixity of the masculine/feminine construct within the confines of terms that themselves belong to the binary, all of those words that carry gender as a heterosexual condition, dimorphic and fixed.

In response to this, in frustration and in utter perplexity at the metaphorical acrobatics involved, one turns to the literal, to the people who are women and who work in architecture. At one level it is as banal as that. Face value. At another level, however, is the instinctive belief that the site with which to grapple, the site that will allow and ultimately best effect the insertion of difference into architecture, is not the space of architecture per se, but the space of the *practice* of architecture. Practice as the niggling daily activity, the mundane, the bodily, the aspect that always disappoints the metaphoric purity of capital-A architecture. Practice as constructed and bounded by all of the (multiple) coordinates that bind us: sexual, cultural, economic, technological, racial, social, and physical.

I have a postcard on which I've become rather dependent in the making of this book. I know very little about it. It is old, probably turn of the century, it comes from Seville and is signed "Cembrano." It shows five remarkably similar women sitting at a round table, each with a closed fan placed before her. Their gazes have a rather disarming way of just missing each other; they are together, but apart.

If you look at this photograph long enough, you suddenly realize that the stripes that make up the wall behind them are in fact a series of mirrors. That this is a photograph of one woman, sitting with her back to us (the camera) at a segment of the table (a fifth) that is completed, as is her company, by the reflections in the mirrors.

Something about this image returns me, whenever lost, to an understanding that is important here. Lost in the face of the questions that beleaguer the subject of women and architecture. Questions like: So *do* women design differently from men? Or, *is* there a feminine architecture? What exactly does it look like? Questions that are dumb at best, and dangerous at worst, that betray a desire for a brand-new (and politically less incorrect) architecture that will save us all, a utopian architecture (as if we hadn't had enough of those). Questions that reveal an architectural economy that would perhaps like to "size up" this latest "new" architecture against its "male" counterpart, quantify it, and perhaps even appropriate it.

But there is more to learn from this postcard. This is an image of a thing at once singular and multiple. An identity and a cacophony. An interior singularity and an external multiplicity.[7] The identity of (the) woman is presented as fragmented, multiple, simultaneous (duplicitous?), collective. This is not a hall of mirrors; it is not about distortion but about a shattering of singularity.

It is an image that attends well to the action of critical practice. That, as critical theory shatters the centrality of the text, so too must critical practice shatter the singular purpose and nature of architectural production into multiple practices for multiple architectures, pertinent to multiple genders.

Lastly, this woman, a container herself, is also in a container; an architecture of mirrors encloses her. The "fourth" wall is the (also glass) lens of the camera observing her. She is contained within the condition of being observed, while observing herself: The trap (read architecture) of autobiography.

Throughout its history, architecture has imported languages from other disciplines, from philosophy, art history, literary criticism, and psychoanalysis. Despite its desire for a single autonomous language, its languages have always been appropriated and consequently "polluted" by other discourses. The recent importation of deconstruction to architecture is typical. However, the very impulse of deconstruction, the question of structure, that made it so eminently, indeed insistently, importable to architecture also made it lock with feminist criticism. The two are now almost inextricably intertwined. It is impossible to speak of one without referring to the other. Yet the elaborate documentation on the action of deconstruction on architecture is marked by the lack of documentation of that of feminist criticism (and related gender theories) on architecture.

One simple and obvious reason for this is the very small number of architects who might choose to apply feminist criticism to architecture: a constituency most easily identifiable as women architects (kindly bear with the crudeness of this statement until I can discuss what it might mean to be a "woman" here). This collection attempts to locate such a constituency (and in particular its critical component) and to examine what constitutes its practice, how this practice is made critical. In doing so exclusively lies the implicit desire to displace the male/female hierarchy so manifest in architectural culture but also takes us back to Derrida and to his positive *insistence* ("J'insiste beaucoup et sans cesse . . ."[8]) on the (ironic) need to reverse the structure that underpins discrimination in order fully to displace a hierarchy. We are reminded that a state of imposed equality alone is not enough to neutralize a hierarchy: the supplementation of a phase that asserts the primacy of the oppressed term is strategically indispensable. However, the supplementary relationship between these two tactics is simultaneous not sequential: "phase" here is structural not chronological.

To broach the question of the term *woman*, we must recognize that the relation between the deconstructive paleonomy "woman" and real women is very slippery. "Woman," as the resisting agent of feminist criticism, acts as the horizon of a critique of certain ideological impositions.[9] However, the evolution of the term "woman" in feminist criticism constantly shuttles between the real and the theoretical: the hypothetical skeleton of this "agent" is fleshed out with experience drawn from real women. The relation between women and "woman" is one of reflexive displacement: each displaces the other. "Woman" is a construct at home neither in the real/empirical world nor in the entirely theoretical world.[10] It is essentially unstable and therefore able (in its application) to displace the fragile specificity of the real toward the powerful universality of the theoretical.

But there is, as Julia Kristeva points out, a need for a more generous (and perhaps literal) understanding of this relationship. A need to allow the two to slide into identity. For women to declare themselves as "woman" in order to make changes for women; just as there is a need to refer to real women's experience in order to evolve this hypothetical "woman."[11] A doubling that continues the tropic tradition (real/theoretical agency) of this term and that allows it to remain the subject of any criticism that desires to subvert sexual repression.

So, though potentially absurd, referring to the direct experiences of women is necessary, as is the inversion of the existing male/female hierarchy (referring exclusively to women), a both absurd and (sadly) strategically necessary way of trying to escape an oppositional system.

Through its relation to deconstruction, the essentially linguistic dilemma of how to displace logocentrism within a language itself trapped in logocentrism becomes, in feminist criticism, how to displace the patriarchy with constructs that themselves reassert the patriarchal. Which of two apparently conflicting strategies to follow—to promote the difference of women, evolving a new language, or to insist that women can fit the (male) human norm and excel at the (patriarchal) normal language?

If we extend the possibility of multiple gender to this conflict, the apparently discrete and dividing structure starts to muddy, and the possibility of a structure that allows the embracing of both strategies simultaneously emerges—of working both within and without the language of logocentrism, elaborating a liminal condition. Both the structure of this book and the selection of contributors attempt to do this, to assert both that women have a special and particular contribution to architecture and that women can do architecture just as men do. It is precisely this diversity, this ability to be central and marginal *simultaneously* that will allow women to expand the territory of architecture.

A critical position is, by necessity, liminal: one must be both an insider and an outsider. A woman who is an architect, through a combination of her gender and profession, is potentially in such a position. Insider by her education, her adoption by and of certain professional institutions; outsider by her difference, her gender-related experience contains grounds for a resistive reading of certain architectural operations. She is able, and almost obliged, to *invent* her practice and to do so critically, in order to test certain accepted aspects of the production of architecture.

Though the critical position here is *located* by gender, its voice cannot be assigned as representing the "feminine." To do so would be to territorialize it and to subscribe to the very categories that it might desire to subvert. Instead, gender is used here to describe a *position* (rather than an attitude) from which critical distance is generated by gender difference.

The selection of authors maps the range of practices of this position and investigates how this diversity might constitute itself. The traditional concepts of practice are replaced by the wider concerns of the activity of the architect, legitimate or illegitimate. The collective presence of the authors represents the full range of architectural practice from the more mainstream to the more marginal, from the intersection of architectural theory and philosophy to the intersection of the building process and technology. The spectrum of viewpoints, cultures, and architectural sites (education, building, theory, history, urban design, visual and performance arts) encompassed portrays a diversification of practice for women architects.

In the juxtaposing of "builders" and "theorists" is an attempt to close the constructed gap between theory and practice and implicitly to call into question the *existence* of this "gap" made manifest in so much architectural representation. Underpinning this is a desire to portray the interdependence of theory and practice in the work of the contributors and to examine the conditions of adjacency and simultaneity that truly constitute the practice of architecture.

What emerges from the collection is a curious reflexive relationship: critical architectural practice is both a way for women to enter architecture and a way for architecture to include women, or woman. Like the mirror postcard, the view is cacophonic: a set of different voices (allegory, autobiography, exposition, criticism, narrative) presenting the multiple and fragmented sites of their practices.

Each author has struggled with the existential problem of writing about herself, of documenting who she is and what she does, as she both is and does. Those who build and are accustomed to leaving the text that "explains" their buildings to others have had to invent ways of portraying their practices without breaking the thin yet necessary web that separates guilelessness from self-consciousness. Those cast as "theorists" and accustomed to writing about others (or about themselves through others) have equally struggled with the potential absurdity of autobiography, of writing about themselves (with no other to be filtered through).

Within the space of their texts, some plot the space of their practices while for some the very strategy of the text is the site of the practice. Within this diversity are certain important recurring strategies that recall those of both deconstruction and feminist criticism: a valuing of the metonymic over the metaphoric; a questioning of the role of the author and a consequent mixing of legitimate with illegitimate texts (in the production of "bastard" readings); a reassessment of the concept of boundary as a thing both physical and conceptual, and its transgression, both physically (in construction) and conceptually (via interdisciplinary appropriation and substitution); and lastly, a reconfiguring of certain orders, present in the architecture inherited, that too clearly embody a metaphorical repression of the female (via the feminine)—Euclidean geometry, the structure/ornament hierarchy, and the form/matter hierarchy, to name a few.

These writings can almost be read as a collection of self-portraits of practice, a collective autobiography of practice. A group portrait where each figure paints herself. The junctions between the figures are sometimes clear, other times fuzzy, even jarring, but strangely illuminating: it is through juxtaposition that the strategy of each text/autobiography reveals itself.

In the simplest, crudest terms, this portrait of the practice of woman architects shows that some crisis does arise out of being a woman and working in architecture—whether it takes form through the quiet tenacity of building or the necessarily vocal dismantling of a paradigm—and that the search for identity instigated by this crisis can generate a critical reconstruction of practice and, implicitly, a reconstruction of the production of architecture.

The writings collectively mark the emergence of important critical architectural practices by women. They carry the hope that architecture's inclusion of women will help finally to undermine the theory/practice divide still manifest in architectural culture and dispel the not entirely unconnected genealogical anxiety (architecture/not architecture), allowing their practices to supplement and expand the field as we now understand it.

Notes

1.   Jacques Derrida, "Choreographies," interview with Christie V. McDonald in *Diacritics* 12, no. 2 (Summer 1982): 76.

2.   Percentage of registered women architects in the U.S.: 10.8 percent (American Institute of Architects, 1995); and in the U.K.: 9 percent (Royal Institute of British Architects, 1994). Percentage of registered women physicians in the U.S.: 20 percent (American Medical Association, 1995); and in the U.K.: 28 percent (British Medical Association, 1992). Percentage of women lawyers in the U.S.: 24 percent (American Bar Association, 1990); and in the U.K.: 29 percent (The Law Society, 1994).

3.   In this unraveling, and many more, I am indebted to Jennifer Bloomer's canny and delightful expositions of all that lurks on the inside of architecture. "There is a grand tradition of figuration of the female body as container, as vase, intimately tied to the figuration of the earth as female body, as receptacle. This points toward both creation and the creation of (other) containers, i.e., architecture (which is then also figured as female, a container)." Jennifer Bloomer, "Architecture and the Feminine: Mop-Up Work," *ANY Magazine* 1, no. 4 (January 1994): 8.

4.   I refer here to the legacy of erotic writings about the relationship between the artist (or maker) and the muse, to Rilke's "bridge barely curved that connects the terrible with the tender." A legacy that promotes a heterosexual relation with the muse, so that the possibility of sidestepping this displacement with a homosexual relation is already discouraged. Any relationship other than the heterosexual can only be oblique. Rainer Maria Rilke, "The Unnatural Will to Art," in *The Modern Tradition: Backgrounds of Modern Literature*, ed. Richard Ellmann and Charles Feidelson (New York: Oxford University Press, 1965), 24.

5.   Similarly, one could argue the same of sexuality—unstable sexuality may evade the grasp of a gendered ideology—but this then introduces the question of the relation between gender and sexuality, another even longer thread that I will drop here, knowing that none of these threads can be truly dropped without getting into serious trouble later. I'm talking about spontaneous unraveling of carefully tied knots.

6.   Multiple gender is briefly introduced here as a way out of the blind alley presented and as a reaction to the alternative (fixed and symmetrical) scenario of the neuter. For further elucidation on multiple gender, a subject not easily made brief, please see: *Third Sex Third Gender: Beyond Sexual Dimorphism in Culture and History*, ed. Gilbert Herdt (New York: Zone Books, 1994); and *The Last Sex: Feminism and Outlaw Bodies*, ed. Arthur Kroker and Marilouise Kroker (New York: St. Martin's Press, 1993).

7.   But as Catherine Ingraham reminds us so well in this volume ("Losing it in Archᵢₜecture: Object Lament"), the relationship of interiority and exteriority is never simple. The exterior is already implied in the interior and vice versa. How many selves does the real woman in this postcard feel she has? Is the photographer trying to tell us something

about her? And these reflections, are they surface women only? Do they have an interiority?

8. *I strongly and incessantly insist on the necessity of this phase of reversal, which people have perhaps too swiftly sought to discredit.* To do justice to this necessity is to recognize that in a classical philosophical opposition we are not dealing with the peaceful coexistence of a *vis-à-vis,* but rather with a violent hierarchy. One of the two terms governs the other (axiologically, logically, etc.), or has the upper hand. To deconstruct the opposition, first of all, is to overturn the hierarchy at a given moment. To overlook this phase of overturning is to forget the conflictual and subordinating structure of opposition. Therefore one might proceed too quickly to a *neutralization* that *in practice* would leave the previous field untouched, leaving one no hold on the previous oposition, thereby preventing any means of *intervening* in the field effectively.

Derrida, *Positions,* trans. Alan Bass (Chicago: University of Chicago Press, 1981), 41. Emphasis (first sentence only) indicates my translation of first sentence of passage omitted from English edition: "J'insiste beaucoup et sans cesse sur la nécessité de cette phase de renversement qu'on a peut-être trop vite cherché à discréditer." Jacques Derrida, *Positions* (Paris: Minuit, 1972), 56–57.

9. Namely that of sexual identity, but also of representation and the subject.

10. Of further complexity is the way in which the term *woman* reintroduces a "femininity" that tests the feminine of the masculine/feminine construct. Femininity, "as real otherness, is uncanny in that it is not the opposite of masculinity but that which subverts the very opposition of masculinity and femininity." Shoshana Felman writing about Balzac's *La Fille aux Yeux d'Or* in "Rereading Femininity," *Yale French Studies,* no. 62 (1981): 42.

11. The belief that "one is a woman" is almost as absurd and obscurantist as the belief that "one is a man." I can say "almost" because there are many goals that women can achieve: freedom of abortion and contraception, day-care centers for children, equality. . . . Therefore we must use "we are woman" as an advertisement or slogan for our demands. On a deeper level however, a woman is not something one can "be"; it does not even belong to the order of *being.* . . . By "woman" I understand what cannot be represented, what is not said, what remains above and beyond nomenclatures and ideologies. There are certain "men" who are familiar with this phenomenon; it is what some modern texts never stop signifying: testing the limits of language and sociality—the law and its transgression, mastery and (sexual) pleasure—without reserving one for males and the other for females.

Julia Kristeva, interview in "La Femme, ce n'est jamais ça," *Tel Quel,* no. 59 (1974): 20–21. English edition: "Woman Cannot Be Defined," in *New French Feminisms,* ed. Elaine Marks and Isabelle de Courtivron (Amherst: University of Massachusetts Press, 1980) 137–38.

THE ARCHITECT
RECONSTRUCTING HER PRACTICE

Chapter 1   **BATTLE LINES: E.1027**   Beatriz Colomina

Anger is perhaps the greatest inspiration in those days when the
individual is separated in so
many personalities. Suddenly
one is all in one piece.

—*Eileen Gray, 1942*

Francesca Hughes has asked us to do something of what we usually do and at the same time to reflect on that very practice. This is a very difficult thing to do. If you think about how you ride a bicycle, you may fall off. At the same time, rethinking the practice of history is what I usually do. History is always a practice of reconstruction. It reconstructs other practices and in so doing reconstructs itself. But it is difficult to talk about this reconstruction because it does not always follow a recognizable pattern. Indeed, every time is different. Research is something of which we are never completely in control. It leads us somewhere, but never to the place we thought we were going.

This paper, for example, grew out of an uncontrollable footnote in my earlier book *Privacy and Publicity.* It was in the chapter "Photography," which in its embryonic form was published in a catalogue edited by Stanislaus von Moos in Zürich, *L'Esprit Nouveau: Le Corbusier und die Industrie 1920–1925.* Von Moos had commissioned me to write that piece; he even gave me the title: "Le Corbusier and Photography." In the end the article was not only about Le Corbusier's use of photography but also, and I believe more importantly, about the way in which photography marks the emergence of a new sense of space, a new architecture, in which interior and exterior are no longer clear-cut divisions—as they were in the model of the camera obscura, the model of the room with a view. In this new sense of space, the traditional distinctions between inside and outside have become profoundly blurred, transforming the role of the architect and modes of subjectivity.

This paper springs from that original article, not simply by taking up where the other one left off but by way of an explosion in one of its footnotes. Because I have omitted from this account of the article, of its history, that there was something about it that always bothered me, but I could not put my finger on it until I was preparing the manuscript for *Privacy and Publicity*, and at a certain point, very late in the process actually (I had even written the introduction; I was ready to go), I found myself rewriting the chapter. First, the footnote started to get bigger and bigger until it reached that point where it would not remain there and jumped into the main text, where, of course, there was more room to move, and it kept growing, until it was really threatening to take over. Eventually I had to remind myself that this kind of thing always happens when you are working on a book and that while there may have been a point to what I was writing, it was effectively acting as a block to finishing the project. So I closed the book, after performing some surgery to remove the growth. And, of course, at the first opportunity it returned, where I least expected.

I was actually working on the seemingly unrelated question of "horizon," a theme that has preoccupied me for some time, and suddenly I found myself back in the space of that footnote. The horizon had become the site for my ongoing obsession, an obsession on which I would like to dwell here. The question of horizon had sent me back to Martin Heidegger's essay "Building, Dwelling, Thinking," written in 1952 and much cited in architectural discourse:

What the word for space, *Raum*, *Rum*, designates is said by its ancient meaning. *Raum* means a place cleared or freed for settlement and lodging. A space is something that has been made room for, something that is cleared and free, namely within a boundary, Greek *peras*. A boundary is not that at which something stops but, as the Greeks recognized, the boundary is that from which something *begins its presencing*. That is why the concept is that of *horismos*, that is, the horizon, the boundary. Space is in essence that for which room has been made, that which is let into its bounds.[1]

The horizon is an interior. It defines an enclosure. In its familiar sense, it marks a limit to the space of what can be seen, which is to say, it organizes this visual space into an interior. The horizon makes the outside, the landscape, into an inside. How can that happen? Only if the "walls" that enclose the space cease to be thought of (exclusively) as solid pieces of material, as stone walls, as brick walls. The horizon organizes the outside into a vertical plane, that of vision. Shelter is provided by the horizon's ability to turn the threatening world of the "outside" into a reassuring picture. But Heidegger repeatedly opposes the transformation of the world into a picture, a "world picture." In *The Metaphysical Foundations of Logic*, he makes even more explicit the idea that the horizon *is* an enclosure but also quickly dismisses the primacy of vision implied in the familiar sense of horizon: "We understand 'horizon' to be the circumference of the field of vision. But horizon, from ὀρίζειν, is not at all primarily related to looking and intuiting, but by itself means simply that which delimits, encloses, the *enclosure*." [2] Before vision, the horizon is a boundary, an enclosure, an architecture.

The way we think about architecture is always organized by the way we think about boundaries. Traditionally it is a matter of walls dividing inside from outside, public from private, and so on. With modernity there is a displacement of the traditional sense of an inside as an enclosed space established in opposition to the outside. All boundaries are shifting. This becomes manifest everywhere: in the city, of course, but also in the technologies that define the space of the city: the railroad, newspapers, photography, electricity, advertisements, reinforced concrete, glass and steel architecture, the telephone, film, radio . . . war. Each can be understood as a mechanism that disrupts the older boundaries between inside and outside, public and private, night and day, depth and surface, here and there, street and interior, and so on. Today, the boundaries defining space are first and foremost an effect of the media (and not exclusively visual media; think, for example, about the space of sound: radio, the telephone, the walkman). The status of the wall has changed.

Throughout this century, this disturbance of boundaries has often been understood as a threat to identity, a loss of self. In talking about horizons, and in condemning their displacement by modern technologies, Heidegger was elaborating Nietzsche's claim that "a living thing can be healthy, strong and fruitful only when bounded by a horizon. . . . A man . . . sickens and collapses [if] the lines of his horizon are always restlessly changing." [3] Modern man, then, will indeed be sick. With every new technology new sicknesses are identified. The idea of modernity can never be separated from the idea of sickness. Even space itself, or more precisely the absence of boundaries, produces sickness. At the turn of the century, urban theorists like Camillo Sitte criticized modern town planning for its failure to institute boundaries. Without a clear horizon, he said, the modern dweller suffers from new nervous disorders such as agoraphobia.[4]

But these sicknesses are almost always phantasmatic. The identity of the supposedly unified self threatened by the displacement of the horizon is itself suspect and must be interrogated. This interrogation must address architectural discourse since the question of horizon is, from the beginning, an architectural question.

1952. The same year that Heidegger published "Building, Dwelling, Thinking," the Spanish architect José Luis Sert, then president of the Congrès Internationaux d'Architecture Moderne (CIAM), opened the eighth congress, "The Heart of the City," devoted to "the core," with a long quotation from José Ortega y Gasset's *The Revolt of the Masses*:

For in truth the most accurate definition of the *urbs* and the *polis* is very like the comic definition of a cannon. You take a hole, wrap some steel wire tightly round it, and that's your cannon. So the *urbs* or the *polis* starts by being an empty space, the *forum*, the *agora*, and all the rest are just means of fixing that empty space, of limiting its outlines. The *polis* is not primarily a collection of habitable dwellings, but a meeting place for citizens, a space set apart for public functions. The city is not built, as is the cottage or the *domus*, to shelter from the weather, and to propagate the species—these are personal, family concerns—but in order to discuss public affairs. Observe that this signifies nothing less than the invention of a new kind of space, much more new than the space of Einstein. Till then only one space existed, that of the open country, with all the consequences that this involves for the existence of man. The man of the fields is still a sort of vegetable. His existence, all that he feels, thinks, wishes for, preserves the listless drowsiness in which the plant lives. The great civilizations of Asia and Africa were, from this point of view, huge anthropomorphic vegetations. But the Greco-Roman decides to separate himself from the fields, from Nature, from the geo-botanic cosmos. How is this possible? How can man withdraw himself from the fields? Where will he go, since the earth is one huge, unbounded field? Quite simply; he will mark off a portion of this field by means of walls, which set up an enclosed finite space over against amorphous, limitless space. Here you have the public square. It is not like the house, an "interior" shut in from above, as are the caves which exist in the fields, it is purely and simply the negation of the fields. The square, thanks to the walls which enclose it, is a portion of the countryside which turns its back on the rest, eliminates the rest, and sets up in opposition to it.[5]

The *urbs* is "like" a cannon. The city is "like" a military weapon. This was not a casual example. War was written all over this congress and its idea of public space. But what kind of war? Most literally, it was World War II. The end of the war found many CIAM architects involved in the task of replanning central areas of bombed-out cities. They saw themselves as heart surgeons, trying to reconstruct vital organs of the city. From this came a preoccupation with the city and with "public space," which they understood as a place of public gathering, both in the traditional sense of public squares, promenades, cafés, etc. and also in what they saw as its most modern counterparts: railroad stations, bus terminals, landing strips. But also from this came a clear, almost phobic opposition to the new means of communications, which were already redefining the sense of public: "Radio, movies, television and printed information are today absorbing the whole field of communication. When these elements are directed by a few, the influence of these few over the many may become a menace to our freedom."[6] The media were identified with war, which is not surprising given their crucial role during the Second World War. Underlying this, however, was the common assumption that the public domain is the domain of violence, whether overt or latent, an assumption that still has currency today. Domestic violence is silenced, unrepresented. But isn't this silencing, this lack of representation, itself violent?

But CIAM 8 was not simply declaring war against the media. Sert insisted on bringing the media into the public square (movies, television screen, radio, loudspeakers) and in so doing turning, in his words, public space into "balconies from where [the public] could watch the whole world."[7] Note that the balcony is an element from domestic architecture, a place for both looking and being looked at. To say that public space is a balcony is already to recognize that the public is not so much a negation of the interior, as in the quotation from Ortega y Gasset, as an occupation of its traditional boundary: the wall. To be in public is to be inscribed in the limit of the interior, inscribed in order to "watch the whole world" (a sense familiar to us today in the commonplace idea that to occupy public space is to be at home watching TV). Far from declaring war on the media, Sert was installing it.

The real war here is architectural. The very separation between public and private, inside and outside, is itself violent in Ortega y Gasset's passage. The public is established "in opposition," "against," "as negation"; "it turns its back." These terms mark a certain hostility. Public space is produced by a violent effacement of the private. But here, returning to Ortega y Gasset's cannon, what is wrapped around the hole that is public space are the interiors excluded from it. The cannon is therefore constructed out of domestic spaces. It is not that public space is violent and the "interior" is safe. The interior is the steel wire of the cannon. It is the very substance of the weapon. The interior is therefore precisely the possibility of the violence that becomes visible outside it.

E.1027. A modern white house is perched on the rocks, a hundred feet above the Mediterranean Sea, in a remote place, Roquebrune at Cap Martin. The site is "inaccessible and not overlooked from anywhere."[8] No road leads to this house. It was designed and built by Eileen Gray for Jean Badovici and herself between 1926 and 1929. Eileen Gray named the house E.1027: E for Eileen, 10 for J (the tenth letter of the alphabet), 2 for B and 7 for G. They both

Avenue des Champs Elysées, Paris. (*CIAM 8: The Heart of the City*, ed. Jaqueline Tyrwhitt et al. [New York: Pellegrini and Cudahy, 1952],9.)

lived there most of the summer months, until Eileen Gray built her own house in Castellar in 1934. After Badovici's death in 1956, the house was sold to the Swiss architect Marie Louise Schelbert. She found the walls riddled with bullet holes. The house had clearly been the site of considerable violence. In a 1969 letter, she comments on the state of the house: "Corbu did not want anything repaired and urged me to leave it as it is as a reminder of war."[9] But what kind of war? Most obviously, it was World War II. The bullet holes are wounds from the German occupation. But what violence was there to the house before the bullets, and even before the inevitable relationship of modern architecture to the military? And anyway, to start with, what is Le Corbusier doing here? What brings him to this isolated spot, this remote house that will eventually be the site of his own death?

"As a young man he had traveled in the Balkans and the near East and had made sketches of strange, inaccessible places and scenes. It was perhaps through a natural, anti-romantic reaction of maturity that later, as a Purist, he proposed to paint what was duplicable and near-at-hand."[10] We will have to go back to Le Corbusier's earlier travels, to the "strange, inaccessible places and

Eileen Gray. E.1027, Roquebrune-Cap Martin. 1926–29. View from the sea. (Eileen Gray Archives, London)

scenes" that he had conquered through drawing—at the very least, to Le Corbusier's trip to Algiers in the spring of 1931. First encounter in what would become a long relationship to this city, or in Le Corbusier's words: "Twelve years of uninterrupted study of Algiers."[11] By all accounts, this study began with his drawing of Algerian women. He said later that he had been "profoundly seduced by a type of woman particularly well built" of which he made many nude studies.[12] He also acquired a large collection of colored postcards representing naked women surrounded by accoutrements from the Oriental bazaar. Jean de Maisonseul (later director of the Musée National des Beaux-Arts in Algiers), who as an eighteen-year-old boy had guided Le Corbusier through the Casbah, recalled their tour: "Our wanderings through the side streets led us at the end of the day to the rue Kataroudji where he [Le Corbusier] was fascinated by the beauty of two young girls, one Spanish and the other Algerian. They brought us up a narrow stairway to their room; there he sketched some nudes on—to my amazement—some schoolbook graph paper with colored pencils; the sketches of the Spanish girl lying both alone on the bed and beautifully grouped together with the Algerian turned out accurate and realis-

Le Corbusier. *Cahiers de dessin* no. 10. 1917. (*Le Corbusier une encyclopedie*, Paris: Centre Georges Pompidou, 1987, 479)

tic; but he said that they were very bad and refused to show them." [13] Le Corbusier filled three notebooks of sketches in Algiers that he later claimed were stolen from his Paris atelier. Ozenfant denied it, saying that Le Corbusier himself either destroyed or hid them, considering them a "secret d'atelier." [14] The Algerian sketches and postcards appear to be a rather ordinary instance of the ingrained fetishistic appropriation of women, of the East, of "the other." Yet Le Corbusier, as Samir Rafi and Stanislaus von Moos have noted, turned this material into "preparatory studies for and the basis of a projected monumental figure composition, the plans for which seem to have preoccupied Le Corbusier during many years, if not his entire life." [15]

From the months immediately following his return from Algiers until his death, Le Corbusier seems to have made hundreds and hundreds of sketches on yellow tracing paper by laying it over the original sketches and retracing the contours of the figures. (Ozenfant believed that Le Corbusier had redrawn his own sketches with the help of photographs or postcards.) [16] He also exhaustively studied Delacroix's famous painting *Femmes d'Alger*, producing a series of sketches of the outlines of the figures in this painting, divested of their "exotic clothing" and the "Oriental decor." [17] Soon the two projects merged: he modified the gestures of the Delacroix figures, gradually making them correspond to the figures in his own sketches. Le Corbusier said that he would have called the final composition *Femmes de la Casbah*. [18] In fact, he never finished it. He kept redrawing it. That the drawing and redrawing of these images became a lifetime obsession already indicates that something was at stake. This became even more obvious when in 1963–64, shortly before his death, Le Corbusier, unhappy with the visible aging of the yellow tracing paper, copied a selection of twenty-six drawings onto transparent paper and symptomatically, for someone who kept everything, burned the rest. [19]

But the process of drawing and redrawing the *Femmes de la casbah* reached its most intense, if not hysterical, moment when Le Corbusier's studies found their way into a mural that he completed in 1938 in E.1027. Le Corbusier referred to the mural as *Sous les pilotis* or *Graffite à Cap Martin*, and sometimes he also labeled it *Assemblage des trois femmes*. According to Schelbert, Le Corbusier "explained to his friends that 'Badou' [Badovici] was depicted on the right, his friend Eileen Gray on the left; the outline of the head and the hairpiece of the sitting figure in the middle, he claimed, was 'the desired child, which was

never born.'"[20] This extraordinary scene, a defacement of Eileen Gray's architecture, was perhaps even an effacement of her sexuality. For Eileen Gray was
openly gay, her relationship to Badovici notwithstanding. And insofar as Badovici is here represented as one of the three women, the mural may reveal as
much as it conceals. It is clearly a "theme for a psychiatrist," as Le Corbusier's
Vers une architecture said of the nightmares with which people invest their
houses[21]—particularly if we also take into account Le Corbusier's obsessive relationship to this house as manifest (and this is only one example of a complex
pathology) in his quasi-occupation of the site after World War II, when he built
a small wooden shack (the Cabanon) for himself at the very limits of the adjacent property, right behind Eileen Gray's house. He occupied and controlled
the site by overlooking it, the cabin being little more than an observation platform, a sort of watchdog house. The imposition of this appropriating gaze is

Eugène Delacroix. *Femmes d'Alger
dans leur appartement.* 1833. Oil on
canvas. Musée du Louvre, Paris. (Photo
R.M.N.)

Le Corbusier. *Etude d'après les Femmes d'Alger de Delacroix.* 50 × 64.5 cm. Chinese ink and colored pencil on tracing paper. Private collection, Paris (Samir Rafi, "Le Corbusier et les Femmes d'Alger," *Revue d'Histoire et Civilisation du Maghreb* [January 1968]: 58–61)

Le Corbusier. *Three Women (Graffite à Cap Martin).* 1938. Mural in Eileen Gray's house E.1027, Roquebrune-Cap Martin. (Alfred Roth, *Begegnungen mit Pionieren* [Basel: Birkhauser, 1973], 119)

even more brutal if we remember that Eileen Gray had chosen the site because it was, in Peter Adam's words, "inaccessible and not overlooked from anywhere." But the violence of this occupation had already been established when Le Corbusier painted the murals in this house (there were eight altogether) without Eileen Gray's permission (she had already moved out). She considered it an act of vandalism; indeed, as Adam put it, "It was a rape. A fellow architect, a man she admired, had without her consent defaced her design."[22]

The defacement of the house went hand in hand with the effacement of Eileen Gray as an architect. When Le Corbusier published the murals in his *Oeuvre complète* (1946) and in *L'Architecture d'Aujourd'hui* (1948), Eileen Gray's house was referred to as "a house in Cap-Martin"; her name was not even mentioned.[23] Le Corbusier ended up, later on, getting credit for the design of the house and even for some of its furniture.[24] Still today the confusion continues, with many writers attributing the house to Badovici alone, or at best, to Badovici and Eileen Gray, and some still suggesting that Le Corbusier had collaborated on the project. Eileen Gray's name does not figure, even as footnote, in most histories of modern architecture, including the most recent and ostensibly critical ones.

"What a narrow prison you have built for me over a number of years, and particularly this year through your vanity," Badovici wrote to Le Corbusier in 1949 about the whole episode (in a letter that Adam thinks may have been dictated by Eileen Gray herself).[25] Le Corbusier's reply is clearly addressed to Eileen Gray: "You want a statement from me based on my worldwide authority to show—if I correctly understand your innermost thoughts—to demonstrate 'the quality of pure and functional architecture' which is manifested by you in the house at Cap Martin, and has been destroyed by my pictorial interventions. OK, you send me some photographic documents of this manipulation of pure functionalism. . . . Also send some documents on Castellar, this U-boat of functionalism; then I will spread this debate in front of the whole world."[26] Now Le Corbusier was threatening to carry the battle from the house into the newspapers and architectural periodicals. But his public position completely contradicted what he had expressed privately. In 1938, the same year he went on to paint the mural *Graffite à Cap Martin*, Le Corbusier had written a letter to Eileen Gray, after spending some days in E. 1027 with Badovici, where he acknowledges not only her sole authorship but also how much he likes the house:

"I am so happy to tell you how much those few days spent in your house have made me appreciate the rare spirit which dictates all the organization, inside and outside, and gives to the modern furniture—the equipment—such dignified form, so charming, so full of spirit."[27]

Why, then, did Le Corbusier vandalize the very house he loved? Did he think that the murals would enhance it? Certainly not. Le Corbusier had repeatedly stated that the role of the mural in architecture is to "destroy" the wall, to dematerialize it. In a letter to Vladimir Nekrassov in 1932, he writes: "I admit the mural not to enhance a wall, but on the contrary, as a means to violently destroy the wall, to remove from it all sense of stability, of weight, etc."[28] The mural for Le Corbusier is a weapon against architecture, a bomb. "Why then to paint on the walls . . . at the risk of killing architecture?" he asks in the same letter, and then answers: "It is when one is pursuing another task, that of telling stories."[29] So what then is the story that he so urgently needs to tell with *Grafitte à Cap Martin?*

We will have to go back once more to Algiers. In fact, Le Corbusier's complimentary letter to Eileen Gray, sent from Cap Martin on April 28, 1938,

Le Corbusier. Cabanon. 30 December, 1951. One of the first sketches (Le Corbusier, *Modulor I and II*, [Cambridge, Mass.: Harvard University Press, 1986], 241. Fondation Le Corbusier)

bears the letterhead: Hôtel Aletti Alger. Le Corbusier's violation of Eileen Gray's house and identity is consistent with his fetishization of Algerian women. One might even argue that the child in this mural reconstitutes the missing (maternal) phallus, whose absence, Freud argues, organizes fetishism. In these terms, the endless drawing and redrawing is the scene of a violent substitution that in Le Corbusier would seem to require the house, domestic space, as prop. Violence is organized around or through the house. In both circumstances (Algiers and Cap Martin) the scene starts with an intrusion, the carefully orchestrated occupation of a house. But the house is in the end effaced (erased from the Algiers drawings, defaced at Cap Martin).

Significantly, Le Corbusier describes drawing itself as the occupation of a "stranger's house." In his last book, *Creation is a Patient Search*, he writes: "By working with our hands, by drawing, we enter the house of a stranger, we are enriched by the experience, we learn."[30] Drawing, as has often been noted, plays a crucial part in Le Corbusier's appropriation of the exterior world. He repeatedly opposes his technique of drawing to photography: "When one travels and works with visual things—architecture, painting or sculpture—one uses one's eyes and draws, so as to fix deep down in one's experience what is seen. Once the impression has been recorded by the pencil, it stays for good—entered, registered, inscribed. The camera is a tool for idlers, who use a machine to do their seeing for them."[31] Statements such as this have gained Le Corbusier the reputation of having a phobia for the camera—despite the crucial role of photography in his work. But what is the specific relation between photography and drawing in Le Corbusier?

The sketches of the Algerian women were not only redrawings of live models but also redrawings of postcards. One could even argue that the construction of the Algerian women in French postcards, widely diffused at the time,[32] would have informed Le Corbusier's live drawings in the same way that, as Zeynep Çelik notes, Le Corbusier precisely reenacts the images of foreign cities (Istanbul or Algiers, for example) constructed by postcards and tourist guides when he actually enters these cities. In these terms, he not only "knew what he wanted to see,"[33] as Çelik says, but saw what he had already seen (in pictures). He "entered" those pictures. He inhabits the photographs. The redrawings of the *Femmes d'Alger* are also more likely to have been realized, as von Moos points out, from postcards and reproductions than from the original

Femmes Kabyles. Postcard bought by
Le Corbusier in Algiers in 1931

Le Corbusier. *Deux Femmes Enlacées*.
c. 1932. 24.5 × 32 cm. Pencil and pas-
tel on cardboard. (Fondation Le Corbusier 114)

painting in the Louvre.[34] So what, then, is the specific role of the photographic image as such in the fetishistic scene of the *Femmes de la casbah* project?

The fetish is "pure presence," writes Victor Burgin, "and how many times have I been told that photographs 'lack presence,' that paintings are to be valued *because of their presence!*"[35] This separation between painting and photography organizes the dominant understanding of Le Corbusier's relation to photography. What these accounts seem to ignore is that here the drawing, the handcrafted artistic meditation, is done "after" the photograph: the art reproduction, the postcard, the photograph.

In fact, the whole mentality of the *Femmes de la casbah* drawings is photographic. Not only are they made from photographs, they develop according to a repetitive process in which the images are systematically reproduced on transparent paper, the grid of the original graph paper allowing the image to be enlarged to any scale. This photographic sensibility becomes most obvious with the murals at Cap Martin. Traditionally, they have been understood as a paradigm of Le Corbusier the painter, the craftsman detached from mechanical reproduction, an interpretation to which Le Corbusier himself has contributed with the circulation of that famous photograph of him, naked, working at one of the murals. (Do you realize that this is the only nude image of him that we know? That it had to be here, in this scene, is telling.) What is normally omitted is that *Graffite à Cap Martin* was not conceived on the wall itself. Le Corbusier used an electric projector to enlarge the image of a small drawing onto the 2.5-meter-by-4.0-meter white wall where he etched the mural in black.

They say that, in using black, Le Corbusier was thinking about Picasso's *Guernica* of the year before, and that Picasso, in turn, was so impressed with the mural at Cap Martin that it prompted him to do his own versions of the *Femmes d'Alger*. Apparently, Picasso drew Delacroix's painting from memory and was "frappé" to find out later that the figure that he had painted in the middle, lying down, with her legs crossed, was not in the Delacroix.[36] It was, of course, *Graffitte à Cap Martin* that he remembered, the reclining crossed-legged women (inviting but inaccessible) Le Corbusier's symptomatic representation of Eileen Gray. But if Le Corbusier's mural had so impressed him, why did Picasso choose not to see the swastika inscribed on the chest of the woman on the right? The swastika may be yet one more sign of Le Corbusier's political opportunism. (Remember that the mural was done in 1938.) But the German soldiers, who

Pablo Picasso. Les Femmes d'Alger, 1955 (d'après Delacroix). 114 × 146 cm. Oil on canvas. Collection W. Ganz, New York

occupied the house during World War II, may not have seen the swastika either, for this very wall was riddled with bullet holes, as if it had been the site of some execution.

The mural was a black and white photograph. Le Corbusier's fetish is photographic. After all, photography too has been read in terms of the fetish. Victor Burgin writes: "Fetishism thus accomplishes that separation of knowledge from belief characteristic of representation; its motive is the unity of the subject. The photograph stands to the subject-viewer as does the fetished object. . . . We know we see a two-dimensional surface, we believe we look through it into three-dimensional space, we cannot do both at the same time—there is a coming and going between knowledge and belief."[37]

So if Le Corbusier "enters the house of a stranger" by drawing, could "the house" stand in here for the photograph? By drawing he enters the photograph that is itself a stranger's house, occupying and reterritorializing the space, the city, the sexualities of the other by reworking the image. Drawing on and in photography is the instrument of colonization. The entry to the house of a stranger is always a breaking and entering—there being no entry without force no matter how many invitations. Le Corbusier's architecture depends in some way on specific techniques of occupying yet gradually effacing the domestic space of the other.

Like all colonists, Le Corbusier did not think of it as an invasion but as a gift. When recapitulating his life work five years before his death, he symptomatically wrote about Algiers and Cap Martin in the same terms: "From 1930 L-C devoted twelve years to an uninterrupted study of Algiers and its future. . . . Seven great schemes (seven enormous studies) were prepared *free of charge* during those years." And later, "1938–39. Eight mural paintings (*free of charge*) in the Badovici and Helen Grey house at Cap Martin."[38] No charge for the discharge. Eileen Gray was outraged; now even her name had been defaced. And renaming is, after all, the first act of colonization. Such gifts cannot be returned.

P.S. In 1944, the retreating German Army blew up Eileen Gray's apartment in Menton, having vandalized E.1027 and Tempe à Paiella (her house in Castellar). She lost everything. Her drawings and plans were used to light fires.

P.P.S. On August 26, 1965, the endless redrawing of the *Femmes de la casbah* still unfinished, Le Corbusier went down from E.1027 to the sea and swam to his death.

P.P.P.S. In 1977 a local mason in charge of some work in the house "mistakenly" demolished the mural *Graffite*.[39] I like to think that he did so on purpose. Eileen Gray had spent almost three years living on the site in complete isolation, building the house with the masons, having lunch with them every day. Then again, she did the same thing when building her own house at Castellar. The masons knew her well; in fact, they loved her and hated the arrogant Badovici. They understood perfectly what the mural was about. They destroyed it. In so doing, they showed more enlightenment than most critics and historians of architecture.

P.P.P.P.S. Since then, the mural has been reconstructed in the house on the basis of photographs. It reemerged from its original medium. The occupation continues.

Notes

1. Martin Heidegger, "Building Dwelling Thinking," (1952), in *Poetry, Language, Thought*, trans. Albert Hofstadter (New York: Harper & Row, 1971), 154.

2. Martin Heidegger, *The Metaphysical Foundations of Logic*, trans. Michael Heim (Bloomington: Indiana University Press, 1984), 208.

3. Friedrich Nietzsche, "On the Uses and Disadvantages of History for Life," in *Untimely Meditations*, trans. R. J. Hollingdale (Cambridge: Cambridge University Press, 1983), 63.

4. Camillo Sitte, "City Planning According to Artistic Principles," trans. George R. Collins and Christiane Crasemann Collins, in Collins and Collins, *Camillo Sitte: The Birth of Modern City Planning* (New York: Rizzoli International, 1986), 183.

5. José Ortega y Gasset, *The Revolt of the Masses* (New York: W. W. Norton, 1932), 164–65, as cited by J. L. Sert in "Centres of Community Life," *CIAM 8: The Heart of the City, Towards the Humanization of Urban Life*, ed. J. Tyrwhitt et. al. (New York: Pellegrini and Cudahy, 1952.), 3.

6. Sert, "Centres of Community Life," 6.

7. Ibid., 8.

8. Peter Adam, *Eileen Gray: Architect/Designer* (New York: Harry N. Abrams, 1987), 174.

9. Letter from Marie Louise Schelbert to Stanislaus von Moos, February 14, 1969, as quoted by Stanislaus von Moos, "Le Corbusier as Painter," *Oppositions* 19–20 (1980): 93.

10. James Thrall Soby, "Le Corbusier, Muralist," *Interiors* (June 1948): 100.

11. Le Corbusier, *My Work* trans. James Palmes (London: The Architectural Press, 1960), p. 50.

12. Samir Rafi, "Le Corbusier et 'Les Femmes d'Alger,'" *Revue d'histoire et de civilisation du Maghreb* (Algiers) (January 1968): 51.

13. Letter from Jean de Maisonseul to Samir Rafi, January 5, 1968, as quoted by von Moos, "Le Corbusier as Painter," 89.

14. From several conversations of both Le Corbusier and Ozenfant with Samir Rafi in 1964. As quoted by Rafi, "Le Corbusier et 'Les Femmes d'Alger,'" 51.

15. Von Moos, "Le Corbusier as Painter," 91.

16. Conversation of Ozenfant with Samir Rafi, June 8, 1964, as quoted by Rafi, "Le Corbusier et 'Les Femmes d'Alger,'" 52.

17. Von Moos, "Le Corbusier as Painter," 93.

18. Rafi, "Le Corbusier et 'Les Femmes d'Alger,'" 54–55.

19. Ibid., 60.

20. Letter from Marie Louise Schelbert to Stanislaus von Moos, February 14, 1969, as quoted by von Moos, "Le Corbusier as Painter," 93.

21. Le Corbusier, *Vers une architecture* (Paris: Crès, 1923), 196. The passage here referred to is omitted in the English version of this book.

22. Adam, *Eileen Gray*, 311.

23. See Adam, *Eileen Gray*, 334–35. No caption of the photographs of the murals published in *L'Architecture d'Aujourd'hui* mentions Eileen Gray. In subsequent publications, the house is either simply described as "Maison Badovici" or credited directly to Badovici. The first recognition of Gray as architect since the twenties came from Joseph Rykwert, "Eileen Gray: Pioneer of Design," *Architectural Review* (December 1972): 357–61.

24. For example, in an article entitled "Le Corbusier, Muralist," published in *Interiors* (June 1948), the caption of the murals at Cap Martin reads: "Murals, interior and exterior, executed in sgraffito technique on white plaster, *in a house designed by Le Corbusier and P. Jeanneret, Cap Martin, 1938.*" Still in 1981, in *Casa Vogue*, no. 119 (Milan), the house is described as "Firmata Eileen Gray–Le Corbusier" ("signed Eileen Gray and Le Corbusier"), and an Eileen Gray sofa as "pezzo unico di Le Corbusier" ("unique piece by Le Corbusier"), as quoted by Jean Paul Rayon and Brigitte Loye, "Eileen Gray architetto 1879–1976," *Casabella* 480 (May 1982): 38–42.

25. "Quelle réclusion étroite que m'a faite votre vanité depuis quelques années et qu'elle m'a faite plus particulièrement cette année." Letter from Badovici to Le Corbusier, December 30, 1949, Fondation Le Corbusier, as quoted by Brigitte Loye, *Eileen Gray 1879–1976: Architecture Design* (Paris: Analeph/J. P. Viguier, 1983), 86; English translation in Adam, *Eileen Gray*, 335.

26. "Vous réclamez une mise au point de moi, couverte de mon autorité mondiale, et démontrant—si je comprends le sens profond de votre pensée—'la qualité d'architecture fonctionnelle pure' manifesté par vous dans la maison de Cap Martin et anéantie par mon intervention picturale. D'ac [sic], si vous me fournissez les documents photographiques de cette manipulation fonctionnelle pure: 'entrez lentement'; 'pyjamas'; 'petites choses'; 'chaussons'; 'robes'; 'pardessus et parapluies'; et quelques documents de Castellar, ce sous-marin de la fonctionnalité: Alors je m'efforcerai d'étaler le débat au monde entier." Letter from Le Corbusier to Badovici, Fondation Le Corbusier as quoted in Loye, *Eileen Gray 1879–1976*, 83–84; english translation in Adam, *Eileen Gray*, 335–36.

27. Letter from Le Corbusier to Eileen Gray, Cap Martin, 28 April, 1938, as quoted in Adam, *Eileen Gray*, 309–10.

28. "J'admets la fresque non pas pour mettre en valeur un mur, mais au contraire comme un moyen pour détruire tumultueusement le mur, lui enlever toute notion de stabilité, de poids, etc." Le Corbusier, *Le passé à réaction poétique*, exhib. cat. (Paris: Caisse nationale des Monuments historiques et des Sites/Ministère de la Culture et de la Communication, 1988), 75.

29. "Mais pourquoi a-t-on peint les murs des chapelles au risque de tuer l'architecture? C'est qu'on poursuivait une autre tâche, qui était celle de raconter des histoires." Ibid.

30. Le Corbusier, *Creation is a Patient Search* (New York: Frederick Praeger, 1960), 203.

31. Ibid. 37.

32. About French postcards of Algerian women circulating between 1900 and 1930 see Malek Alloula, *The Colonial Harem* (Minneapolis: University of Minnesota Press, 1986).

33. Zeynep Çelik, "Le Corbusier, Orientalism, Colonialism," *Assemblage* 17 (1992): 61.

34. Von Moos, "Le Corbusier as Painter," 93.

35. Victor Burgin, "The Absence of Presence," in *The End of Art Theory: Criticism and Postmodernity* (Atlantic Highlands, N.J.: Humanities Press International, 1986), 44.

36. Rafi, "Le Corbusier et 'Les Femmes d'Alger,'" 61.

37. Victor Burgin, "Modernism in the Work of Art," *20th Century Studies* 15–16 (December 1976); reprinted in Burgin, *The End of Art Theory*, 19. See also Stephen Heath, "Lessons from Brecht," *Screen* 15, no. 2 (1974): 106 ff.

38. Le Corbusier, *My Work*, 50–51 [my emphasis].

39. Von Moos, "Le Corbusier as Painter," 104.

Chapter 2

REAR WINDOW

Martine De Maeseneer

For men: to convince is to con-
quer without *conception*.

—*Walter Benjamin*[1]

A Prelude

Form has always been a male preserve, as the ambiguous meaning of *erecting* something conceals/reveals: a primary extrovert force. Opposed to form, we are bound to place function as conceptive and female territory, exemplified by one room in particular (the kitchen) where the (house) wife has traditionally been placed.

But any understanding of function as a female territory becomes convoluted very quickly, as both terms are essentially unstable. Since the advent of modernism the meaning of function has been displaced from the concerns of "dwelling" to the far more minimal concerns of machines and (heavenly) motions: the Newtonian rhetoric. However, as the kitchen is also the site of alchemy, it can in a sense be thought of as an allegory of this cold, frigid worldview and of the "overheating" of the Newtonian machine.

The kitchen then, usually located at the back of the house (enter without knocking) provides a way of deviating from the slippery early modern debate of "form" and "function," to the late modern (or better, postmechanical[2]) question of "seeing" and "knowing": seeing representing perceptual space, the preoccupation with one autonomous space, and knowing, conceptual space, space divided into discrete functions and cells by psychological thresholds. Thus the possibility of an architecture in which the question of gender becomes inscribed in the difference between these two properties emerges.

The projects presented here comprise in one way or another exercises on this seeing versus knowing construct and on the delicate problem of how to find a proper architectural language for it. One such language derives from topological play with prepositions integral to architectural nouns such as door, facade, cantilever, room (in Dutch and Flemish), where the role of prepositions as local "invariables that articulate the relationship between things, people, and actions"[3] is allowed to take on new meaning.

Seeing Versus Knowing

How boring it is to concentrate on organization, program, and function when designing a building. Everyone knows that the kitchen is situated next to the dining room, the bathroom next to the bedroom, the toilet . . . They are all inherited relationships. For ten thousand years, houses were built, demolished, and rebuilt on the same foundations. Stone was brought from a nearby quarry, clay dug up from the local subsoil. This led, through countless accumulations, to a blurring of the line dividing foundation from wall. In short, function and form, ground and figure were one and the same substance and belonged to what we could call "the undivided space."[4]

The ideological break between form and function first manifested after the Renaissance (as part of an ongoing process of rationalization), took on massive proportions only at the beginning of this century with industrial, economic, and colonial expansion. This, combined with the consequent dissolving of distance through the development of mass transportation, culminated, inevitably, in the birth of modern architecture.

One icon of modern architecture is, of course, the Villa Savoye, floating above the ground on pilotis. Le Corbusier here was referring to the stern of the ocean liner *Aquitania*, a ship that sailed on international waters (no fixed ground). While in the Villa Stein in Garches, Le Corbusier experimented with regulating lines and right angles, in search of pure and beautiful forms and proportions. The persistent belief in both is that with the discovery of the simple mechanics of the universe "man" suddenly found himself at the brink of unraveling the secrets of life itself. Clearly this attitude, this entire preoccupation with seeing, became central to the architecture of that period. In those euphoric days of social and economic revolution, the split between form and function was simply dismissed as a small pathological effect still to be overcome via rationalization and standardization.

Few, however, noticed within the broader social context that the dichotomy between form and function appeared at the advent of a more fundamental break between seeing and knowing: in the late twenties Werner Heisenberg and his matrix school showed that light can travel both in the form of a particle and a wave. Whenever one tries to measure the momentum of a particle in a given system, its velocity deforms and conversely whenever one tries to measure the velocity, its momentum deforms. The possibility of determining and comprehending our universe via simple and reversible laws was forever lost. Another revelation, implicit in quantum mechanics, is that a particle can "choose" its own way.[5]

The discovery of the Uncertainty Principle, the result of a thought experiment conducted in the closed environment of the laboratory, immediately overthrew the autonomy of the Newtonian visual (read measurable) space-time continuum. The split between knowing and seeing occurred. Meanwhile the rationalization of architecture was in full swing. One could hardly speak of any "uncertainty" there. Reason in modern architecture expressed itself primarily in the form of emancipation from the old vernacular, from the mythical religious yoke: the house became an object for use, made to the measure of the average man. Light, air, and decentralization were put forward as alternatives to the hierarchically centralized house. The romantic image of the furnished, stuffy, spatially wasteful mansion was denounced. This was a period of ideological purification: the bathroom (tellingly) became one of the most important rooms in the house.[6]

On closer inspection, however, we see that the prevailing trend in modern housing is in fact the repression of function. In the already compact living unit the void is introduced (one autonomous space or cell) merely to enhance spaciousness and openness. This is done with no social agenda in mind. "Superfluous" walls are eliminated (to compensate for the loss of actual living space). Dividing walls are reduced in size to an absolute minimum. Spaciousness is expressed by displaying the longest measurable axis:[7] the diagonal, the ramp or staircase crossing the double-height void.

What this modernist obsession with visual, geometric space overlooks is that, apart from the actual measurable space, magnitude and spaciousness are partly generated by the crossing of thresholds between different spaces, cells, and functions and by the number of times one *changes direction* on the way (as in a labyrinth). Often the subtle game of social hierarchy between different cells (psychological or physical) and the resultant conflicts, or lack of conflict, makes the business of habitation livable.[8] Openness in this context is associated with *choice* instead of light and air.[9]

During and immediately after the Second World War, the belief in the great ideal and rationale was finally eclipsed by the great uncertainty. (Doubt after all spurred René Descartes to penetrate the essence of his dualistic philosophy.) Within modernist architecture several distinct shifts took place concerning the seeing/knowing paradigm, with the revival of function as the most important result.[10] Not for long, however.

In the framework of the late twentieth-century "deconstruction" of Newtonian space, a number of mechanisms were tested in order to simulate and conduct deviations from within the modern structure: a computer-generated "stretch and fold" manipulation of a photograph of Henri Poincaré (a famous turn-of-the-century mathematician and propagator of the obsession with pure form and geometry) yielded, after numerous repetitions, only the "same" photograph.[11] Peter Eisenman presents a metaphor of this experiment by having his own photograph folded (somewhat miraculously) into a capital letter C (standing for "cyberspace," I presume).[12] Ultimately neither Eisenman's picture nor his architectural projects on the theme of the fold (Rebstock Park, for example) escape the outcome of the Poincaré experiment: the ideal of a deterministic and measurable world picture still stands.[13] Significantly, the current deconstructionist movement (as far as program and function are concerned) can only raise a minimal consensus, be it that the program is in suspension.

Today the fascination with "seeing" is more conspicuous than ever, partially because of the role that the media has claimed within our society. The broadening of the early modernist "perspective," in which the spectator was still associated with a route to be traveled (a promenade), toward the postmodern "panorama" (the spectacle), has only reduced the dynamic position of the architectural tourist to a state of inertia: standing on an escalator or seated in a chair while being bombarded with images and more images of (among other things) the surrogate city.[14] In this situation the acute danger of mass epilepsy, popularly called "falling sickness" exists. The anticlimax (and probably the only possible climax) approaches when the spectator can no longer map the ever accelerating stream of images.

The functional in architecture, when contrasted with the spectacular—if we stick here to a minor reading of Le Corbusier's notion that "good architecture is written in the ground"—signifies keeping both your feet on the ground.[15] In other words, as long as we have hands, feet, and a mouth to eat, banal elements such as doors, windows, toilets, and all of their related functions will remain a true part of architecture. In many psychological thrillers, precisely these banal architectural elements form a source of great tension (I am thinking of Alfred Hitchcock's *Rear Window*), a point that the discourse of contemporary architecture seems to have passed by—ironic, considering its fascination with image and the cinema.

Topology

In current postmodern discourse, the notion of virtual space is very much in vogue and is associated with the imminent dematerialization of a society focused on spectacle—one autonomous space (the void), one network of visual impulses; everyone is wired up. But to understand the property of knowing, we must shift attention toward the liminal properties of space, the psychological thresholds, interfaces, or barriers that produce many spaces as opposed to the singular, continuous space of seeing. Karl Popper's illustration of the soap bubble and the cloud offers an accurate description of such properties. In the soap bubble, Popper recognizes a soft system with organic as opposed to mechanical characteristics. When the temperature rises, the soap bubble expands. The existence and materialization of systems of this kind depend entirely on the presence of an unstable and permeable boundary (the soap film) that regulates both what is inside (a small cloud) and outside (a large cloud) the bubble. Thus in the case of the soap bubble, one can talk about control, but this control works from both sides, being inherent in the interaction between the inside (local) and the outside (global). In other words, it is entirely dependent on mutual feedback.

In the context of architecture and urbanism, this system presupposes the participation and interaction of many spaces or cells to the extent that it is more useful to speak of a topological rather than an organic system.[16] Coherence in such a cluster of cells (some fall off, some get by) is achieved by local agreement or rules of play developed slowly from below and "contaminated" with the physicality of labor, not from above, in a flash and in abstraction.

Examples of possible topological relations are a cell next to a cell and a cell placed within a cell; these are the subject of experimentation in the following projects in which cell-in-a-cell or cell-next-to-a-cell relations are conceptual devices that carry no predetermined shape or form.

Different questions must be posed to address the shape-making of these relationships. It is no longer a question of ideal forms or true forms or perfect forms, terms that bring back the entire rhetoric of pure intuition and seeing (the Newtonian legacy). Nor is it a question of which language they speak. Rather, one must ask whether these forms "work" or don't work or work critically. If knowing is the domain of the nonform and of an unspectacular architecture, the ultimate question is then, which architecture?

What happens in the design process when I take the rear facade as a recto/verso copy of the front facade (the Lambrecht House)? When I regard the rear facade as an upside down front facade? When I turn one entire house on its side, with an identical upright house put next to it (New Sloten Housing project)? Or what happens when I impose a public level in between the sleeping level and the living level? How does this topographical plan influence the social patterns at stake?

The trick is to avoid the traps of style, form, type, language, metaphor, and structure.

The resulting twist of these apparently playful matters occurs in the interior, in the intermediate and hidden zone where the impact of this reversal of outer surfaces takes effect (Recto-Verso House). In other words, inside is where the event takes place. This leads to the more complex question: How can I exchange the sleeping level (traditionally upstairs) and the living level (traditionally downstairs) without interrupting the hierarchy from public/living to private/sleeping (Van Vaerenbergh House and Croes House)? The possible answers balance precariously on the uncertain relationship between what is seen and what is known.

Constructs such as a cell-in-a-cell, or a cell-next-to-a-cell are archaic, dating from an understanding of space that we have chosen to call the "undivided space"; they were brought about through elaborate trial and error. Possibly this very quality, this long-term endurance, ultimately meant that these principles were unable to adapt to things modern and to the radical change that the latter entailed. This inability led in turn to the collapse of the form/ function alliance. The twentieth-century rise and fall of the machine age (the Second World War stands out as a sad highlight of the failure of the machine age to serve human needs) has blocked any return to a simple reunion of form and function and toward the security of the vernacular house. It is comforting, nonetheless, that we can still refer to this mutant ideological framework.

Cobra and Children's Drawings

Wanting to see the schism between form and function as related to the break between seeing and knowing, we have carefully avoided an alternative line of thinking, the discussion of form (modernist) and figure (postmodernist) so eagerly pursued in the seventies. What distinguishes modern form from post-modern figure is that the former is quickly associated with geometry and measure while the latter is entirely contained within language. The dichotomy between form and figure can similarly (and respectively) extend to that of seeing and knowing.

The trouble with figure, however, is that it originates in art instead of architecture, and moreover in Claude Lévi-Strauss's critique of abstract "high" art (against which modern architecture was accustomed to test itself). Lévi-Strauss states that with the objective of reaching a transcendent true art, art became solely the business of the initiated and the prophetic. As a result it lost its status as a language or communicative medium, so strongly recognizable in primitive art.

When it comes to putting forward an architectural consensus, the issue becomes more complex: on the one hand, where the logical function of art lies in representation and signification (in conformity with Lévi-Strauss's stance, which inspired the 1970s postmodernists), the logical function of architecture is simply and primarily habitation. On the other, by replacing the "mastermind" with a "collective brain" anthropology does not escape from a mechanical world picture. Individual behavior, free will, and choice are equally constrained. In other words, there is little or no exchange between individuals and the group, the local and the global. In anthropology the rule is prior to the event, since the rule is considered to be stored within the collective brain.[17]

We would like here to embrace a minor language and a minor art. Cobra (a contraction of COpenhagen, BRussels, and Amsterdam—note the topography) was a brief but intense art movement in the fifties. Though founded in reaction to the philosophy of abstract "high" art, it did not want to lapse into the representative art then current in schools and academies, which had assumed dogmatic proportions. As a way out, the Cobra movement found inspiration in drawings by children and in the art of the mentally handicapped.[18] A similar return to sources (though less pronounced) occurred in architecture, where experiments were made in topological problems, in a kind of profound introspection, after the Second World War. One example is Le Corbusier's chapel of Ronchamp built near another three-country crosspoint: Switzerland, France, and Germany.

Ronchamp deals with the question of how external surfaces turn inward (partly as a way to erode the autonomy of the early modernist space). One encounters similar topological play in the psychoanalysis of children. According to Jean Piaget, the infant forms preconcepts of separation, proximity, repetition, extension, and enclosure in the earliest stage of the development of its intellect. This leads to the role of the preposition in the child's "minor" use of language.[19] Minor because in the child's case, following Piaget's argument in yet a different context, the equilibrium between the assimilation of individual images of objects (roughly enabling one to distinguish a house—pitched roof, four walls, door, and windows—from a castle—moat, towers, bridge) and the accommodation of general internalized schemes essential for proper communication (a house with a flat roof is still a house) are in a state of flux:[20] a *small* house with a *large, red* overhanging roof, and the *tiniest* door, situated within a *large* wood may not be a house but the abode of a witch. Consequently, when we return again to the functioning of the house, where nouns such as door, roof, and window can be assigned fully contained forms and meanings, prepositions (and we now generalize our argument to the entire field of adjectives: small/large, black/white) excel in their limited ability to name things and to represent. They can hardly speak for themselves. The significance of prepositions (as well as adjectives) is always "relative" to the things, persons, and actions they accompany. But through this relative significance these attributes (prepositions, adjectives, and in the Dutch-Flemish language also postpositions) become particularly valuable as elements of organization and of functioning.[21]

Put differently, these attributes (prepositions) simply stand "open" (or "closed," whenever explicitly required) and are conceptive to contextual elements. Then, as one might suspect, departing from the child's drawing (of the house) with the caricature of front door, window, roof, chimney, the relationships obtained between people, things, and actions are never quite certain.

Annex

In his analysis of La Tourette, to make a statement about frontality, Colin Rowe sets out on his journey via the back alley: "Along the kitchen garden of uncertain extent . . . while approaching the monastery at his flank . . . the architect is displaying a profile rather than a full face. And accordingly, assuming that the expressive countenance of the building must be around the corner,"[22] Rowe quite unexpectedly finds himself at the kitchen entrance. He travels no further. Here too the way into the projects presented is around the back. Literally, in a few cases the front entrance is moved backward (Van Vaerenbergh House), getting physically as well as textually closer to the rear entrance.

Cabrio House The house is constructed out of two identical bowed planes. The vertical bowed plane is grafted onto the forest edge; the horizontal plane relates to the surrounding fields: The house is situated at the dividing line between woods and fields.[23] The most private room, the master bedroom, is concealed from the eye, accommodated in the overlap between the horizontal and vertical planes (a space within a space). From and toward this space, all frontal views are blocked, leaving only diagonal views. By contrast, the remaining rooms emphasize frontal views (e.g., onto the woods).

Next, with reference to children's house drawings (Cabrio is a quasi-anagram of Cobra), chimney, door, window, wall, and carport (the vocabulary of the vernacular house) are all present, albeit disproportionate and caricatured.

The Cabrio House also relates (despite the vernacular elements) to the early modernist Citrohan House by Le Corbusier: *Cabrio* also means "convertible" and perverts the French car that served Le Corbusier's notion of rationalism. *Cabrio* says "comfort" and "cruising." The house resists any single label or picture. It is often frequented by architectural students, and it was broadcast in an art program on television. It has appeared in an encyclopedic yearbook,[24]

Cabrio House, Meise. 1988–93. Night
view. (© Lautwein & Ritzenhoff,
Germany)

Van Backlé Opticians, Brussels. 1989–
90. Shop space. (© Lautwein & Ritzenhoff, Germany)

Croes House and photo studio, Antwerp.
1990. Unbuilt project. Perspective of
double staircase

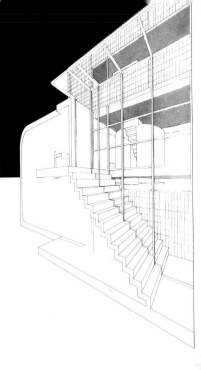

has been incorporated as a curio in a local treasure hunt, and recently appeared in an advertisement for a bank under the slogan: "Such the dream house—Such the Bank."

Van Backlé Optician's Shop The topographical model here is that of a (new) cell slid into an (old) existing cell structure, an apartment building. The area of friction between old and new (the optician's shop forms an extension to an existing pharmacy) accommodates a separate entrance hall. This separation of entrance hall, retail space, and workshop recalls the cellular composition of the "closed" house. However, the walls between the three functions are pierced to allow visual continuity between cells. This generates a contradiction between visual access and psychological barriers. The client will always wait, perhaps somewhat uneasily, in the entrance hall until invited by the optician into the shop.

The theme of classification, initiated by splitting the shop into cells, is further pursued at a smaller scale: the spectacles are stored in vertical racks that roll in and out selectively according to price and type. This prevents the simultaneous viewing of the entire collection and consequent lapse into a mass blur.

Classification is also reiterated in the excessive framing at every scale, framing the notion of seeing itself. Seeing is further brought rhetorically into the picture via the study of (sixteenth-century) optics, by the use of such Renaissance forms as framing pediments and a cupola with an oculus (the eye of God); the intersection of axes and views beneath this oculus divides the space into perfectly symmetrical quadrants, a transcendental form of classification. The study of dynamics (of which the study of optics was the "eye-opener"—the invention of optical instruments and consequent study of planetary motion confirmed the still hypothetical laws of dynamics) is represented in the rolling racks, rotating fitting table, and outsized wheels. The Renaissance palazzo is zoomed in to the scale of, say, a boudoir or a tram stop. (A tram actually stops right in front of the shop and inspired the use of the outsized wheels and folding door at the entrance.)

The design displays an inability to choose between the monumental and the picturesque. The hybrid tram-stop-cum-optician's-shop allegorizes the modernist fascination with ocean liners sailing on international waters (one autonomous space). Here, the metaphor of the tram imposes a local captive dynamism, trapped within the city of Brussels.

Croes House This house and studio for a photographer is situated in the suburbs of Antwerp. Living accommodation is in a duplex above the studio, sleeping in an annex set in the garden. Thus the design inverts the traditional house type. The critical point of this inversion occurs at the double staircase positioned between the main building and the annex. Double, since a public staircase (the exterior half) leading to the living quarters projects through a glass wall to become a private staircase (the interior half), which in turn leads via a detour back down to the sleeping quarters. In spite of the open visual relationship between the staircases, the hierarchical progression from public to private is sustained. The glass wall becomes the ultimate psychological dam.[25]

The cellular composition in the Croes House is manifest in the pattern of annex next to main building (cell-next-to-a-cell) but also in the cell-within-a-cell pattern of the giant central cupboard projected through the separate levels. The three-dimensional cylindrical volume on the first level (containing the bathroom, staircase, and coatroom) becomes a two-dimensional disk (containing a retractable staircase) suspended in the studio. This cupboard projection generates a visual coherence (seen from the outer staircase through the glass wall) not explicitly followed by the structure, causing a split between seeing and structure.

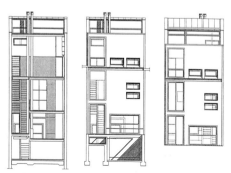

Front Facade/Recto   Rear Facade/Verso

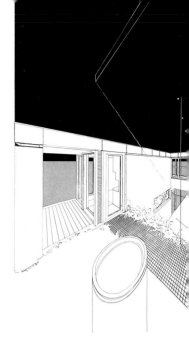

Lambrecht House This row house in Brussels, designed for an art critic and his family, is an exercise in the play of facades and surfaces: the rear facade forms a recto/verso projection of the front facade, an intellectual conceit that refers to the Citrohan House built in Antwerp by young Le Corbusier for the painter René Guillette. In the Citrohan House, however, as in a traditional row house, front and rear facades are symmetrical (not recto/verso) replicas of each other, allowing an interior corridor to link front and back door and implement a linear organization of spaces.

In the Lambrecht House, the recto/verso treatment discourages linear organization. The space splits. Circulation becomes looplike: a core and a boundary. The core, as in the Croes House, is a cupboard like structure projected through several levels. All functions are linked to this, leaving the outer wall entirely free for works of art.

As an extension of the cell-in-a-cell play—the central cupboard—the ground level features a series of outsized table like structures: a cell-next-to-a-cell. One demarcates the dining room, one the garden pavilion, and one the carport (in the preliminary design). This cellular repetition, positioned out, in, and out between back and front garden, asserts an alternative to the vernacular rear-to-front-door passage.

Van Vaerenbergh House This house combines cell-next-to-a-cell and sleeping/living inversion, here derived from embedding the house over its entire length in a three-meter-high embankment. Sleeping takes place at street level; living at garden level.

The insertion of an open cell in between the closed cells allows for an embankment, part of the surrounding slope, to link the rear and front garden *through* the house. It further allows the insertion of a suspended, tilted plane (a token response to a town-planning forty-five-degree roof pitch requirement), which in turn interacts formally with the slope of the embankment (real/abstract). The open cell serves as a carport and entrance gate. A double staircase (inside/outside) attaches to this cell, and, contrary to that in the Croes House, is split running in opposite directions on either side of the cell. Finally, within the same play on ambivalence between real/abstract, open/closed, inside/outside, a free-floating footway connects the living space (main building) with the kitchen (annex) and finds its counterpart in a tunnel running underneath the slope connecting the sleeping areas (seen/hidden).

Sleeping happens on street level, but one has to pass via the outside staircase, across the living room, via the footway, down the interior staircase, and
along the tunnel to reach the sleeping quarters. Despite the sleeping/living
inversion, the traditional hierarchical separation of spaces is maintained by a
split between what is seen and what is known.

Piessens Shoe Import Center The office block consists of two similar volumes, one placed on top of the other and shifted off true. Administration (open
structure) is on the ground level, and the showroom (closed structure) on first
level. The most active zone is the overlap between the two, demarcated by a
circular corridor. Consequently the ground level divides into a core (a cluster
of offices) and an L-shaped peripheral area. The latter contains secondary functions (bathroom, kitchen, refectory, waiting room, patio).

A first, incisive move toward the local is achieved by overlaying the circulation loop with a pinwheel structure consisting of four red volumes and
planes flying out from the center: one element establishes a link with the exterior (the entrance awning); another relates to the showroom (the encased
monumental stairs); a third to the secondary zone (a red beam articulates the

Piessens Shoe Import. Patio on show-room level. (© Lautwein & Ritzenhoff, Germany)

relationship of the owner's wife's office to the L-shaped patio). Finally, a red volume projects over the loading platform, the owner's (husband's) office. A private entry (or exit, as the case may be) is provided here via the underlying carport. The overlap of the ringlike circulation with the pinwheel generates a certain dynamic: all offices are directly and unhierarchically linked to the ring corridor, with the exception of the owner's office, which pierces through and divides this round walk. All offices look out on or are concealed from each other via alternating transparent and opaque (cross-shaped) walls, with exception again of the owner's office, from and into which views are entirely blocked (only a few narrow diagonal slits allow glimpses into and out of the red volume). This entire setting should *imply* that the owner is wholly in control of the business.[26]

In a second move to reduce the scale of the building the composition is made cellular: the building is conceived as a cluster of open/closed cells (shoe boxes). One cell is lifted out of the main cluster to provide a patio on the showroom level and placed next to the building, the caretaker's quarters. The themes of open/closed, global/local, and seen/hidden[27] explored in the previous projects are reiterated here.

They are also employed in the fenestration: holes cut out of the upper closed mass (the showroom) match projections in the solid wall at ground level, positioned behind the continuous glass wall. These projections provide local vertical stitches in a building dominated by horizontal layering.

New Sloten Housing Project (*Sloten I*) A closed competition for a series of eight small islands of housing (each island containing four to eight houses) was organized by the city of Amsterdam as the finale of a large new housing scheme (New Sloten). The site forms a last link, a touchstone, to the old village of Sloten. The problem was how to relate the vernacular and the modern; individual houses with large linear housing; pitched roofs on one hand, flat roofs on the other.

Two types of houses, modern (white) and organic (black), were copulated in a variety of positions relating to length, height, or breadth.[28] This generated a variety of buildings that occupy the middle ground between the individual/collective architectural dichotomy. This coupling shifts attention away from the autonomously designed space toward the interface where the

Sloten I: large island, Amsterdam.
1992. Four elevations of paired-house
types

two houses meet/mate. Mutual entrances are inserted here. Within this context the application of double staircases and living/sleeping inversion proved ideal. In each pair, for instance, it is not evident to the "outsider" which stairs or which entrance leads to which house: The gap between what is seen and what is known is exploited to the maximum advantage of the "insider."

Under the maxim "things are not always what they appear to be" the act of coupling further destabilizes the formal typology of both house types. The organic type, with its references to broad chimneys and cantilevers, becomes no more than an envelope wrapped around a pinwheel of spaces (a modernist motif). Cellular composition, associated with organic architecture, is caricatured by black volumes (mostly the bathrooms) that pierce the flat, blank facade of the white modern type. Play with primary criteria such as wall, roof, chimney, and cell, which constitute the vernacular house, is never far away.

Rear Window | 45

OP-ZIJ (Sloten II) Sloten II, the offspring of Sloten I, is being built on the outermost of the eight islands: The Dutch word OP-ZIJ means both "a-side" and "up-side" in English. Within the OP-ZIJ project, the ZIJ-house (side) is a copy of the OP-house (up) turned on its side. Further, the split-level in the OP-house repeats in the receding facade of the ZIJ-house.[29] In the OP-house the section

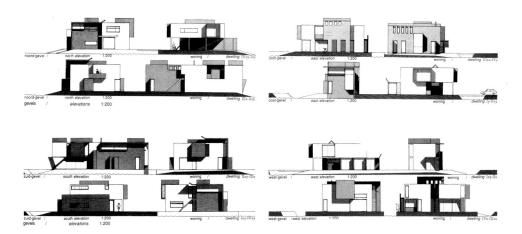

dominates, albeit restricted to two and a half levels; similarly, in the ZIJ-house, the plan is dominant.

The topological play between up and side also defines the window and wall sequences. Two principles govern: all wall surfaces on the orthogonal grid, imposed on the island and spread out from the ZIJ-house, are white. All wall surfaces shifted from the orthogonal grid and spread out from the OP-house are black. In all shifted wall sequences windows are inserted in an up-standing (vertical) manner. In all orthogonal wall sequences, windows are horizontal. Topological play also occurs in the placement of the four pairs of houses on the island. The OP-house becomes the inner house and focuses perspectively on the water surrounding the island. The ZIJ-house becomes the outer house and surveys in a panoramic manner the surrounding fields.

OP-ZIJ is also the name of a feminist magazine in the Netherlands; here it translates as "Step aside, make room!"

Notes

1. Walter Benjamin, "One-Way Street," in *Reflections: Essays, Aphorisms, Autobiographical Writings*, ed. and introd. Peter Demetz (New York: Schocken Books, 1986), 63 [my emphasis].

2. A term coined by Ilya Prigogine and Isabelle Stengers, *Order out of Chaos: Man's New Dialogue with Nature* (London: Flamingo Paperbacks, 1986). First published in France in 1979 under the title *La Nouvelle Alliance.*

3. *Verschueren Dictionary*, (Antwerp: Standaard Vitgeverij, 9th ed., 1991), 2135.

4. Cf. "The In-di-visible Matrix Space," in *Martine De Maeseneer: The In-di-visible Space*, exhib. cat. (Antwerp: Singel Gallery, 1993).

5. Arthur I. Miller, "On the Limitations of the Imagination," in *Imagery in Scientific Thought* (Cambridge: MIT Press, 1986), 153, 221, 250–54, 259. See also David C. Cassidy, "Hiesenberg, Uncertainty and the Quantum Revolution," *Scientific American* Vol. 266, no. 5. (May 1992): 64–70.

6. According to Elizabeth Wilson, one argument behind building garden cities in the nineteenth century was to keep women away from the city: this motive was adopted by the modernist *unités*. The term *public women* derives from this period and refers to all women who move about and/or live in the city without male company. Interestingly one postcard in particular was used to illustrate this nineteenth-century male attitude toward (public) women: it shows a group of women visiting the underground sewers in Paris. See Elizabeth Wilson, "Women in the City," lecture given at the Singel Gallery, Antwerp, September 22, 1993; see also idem, *The Sphinx in the City* (London: Virago Press, 1991), 18.

7. In Le Corbusier, the use of the balustrade element to diagonally cut the image that illustrates the interior of the mass-produced artisans' dwellings is symptomatic of this strategy. Le Corbusier, *Towards a New Architecture* (New York: Dover Publications, 1986), 255. First published in France in 1923 under the title *Vers une architecture* in Le Corbusier's own avant-garde magazine *L'Esprit Nouveau*.

8. "In moments of despair [reflections on the suicide of her child] certain compartments come to exist in oneself, in one you can work, in one you can sleep, in one you can eat and clean the house." Monika Van Paemel, interview in OP-ZIJ, no. 10 (October 1993): 59.

9. On the properties of choice see Robin Evans, "The Developed Surface: An enquiry into the brief life of an eighteenth century drawing technique," *9H*, no. 8 (London) (1989): 147:

    It is worth bearing in mind that informality, the word that was used in the eighteenth and nineteenth century to describe the new domestic geography, was not an abolition of formality but an alternative constitution of relations between many diverse things. For instance, in order to escape the tyranny of obsequious, unified conversation, the empty space of the room, which offered a sort of freedom of its own, was overrun by the furniture which then rendered the definition of action far more specific than before.

10. One example is the monastery of La Tourette, designed by Le Corbusier according to the rule of Saint Augustine of the Dominican Community: "When you go to table, until you stand up again listen to the regular reading without sound and without dispute, for you shall take in nourishment not only through your mouth, but your ears also shall be hungry for the word of God." Analogously Le Corbusier made sure that circulation within the building passes through relatively narrow corridors (the *Kreuzgang*), which hardly encourages communication, only to end up at the main functions—the library, the refectory, the church—all retreats for study, contemplation, and prayer. Le Corbusier managed to design a building that is apparently labyrinthine and inaccessible to the outside world yet is perfectly intelligible within the context of religion and the Monk's ongoing daily life. See Anton Henze, *La Tourette: The Le Corbusier Monastery* (London: Percy Lund Humphries & Co, 1986), 8.

11. J. P. Cruthfield et al., "Chaos," *Scientific American* (December 1986): 38–39.

12. Ole Bouman, "Salt Peter in My Wounds—The Eisenman Excess," *Archis* 2–94 (The Netherlands Architecture Institute, Rotterdam, in association with C. Misset Publishers, Doetinchem, 1994), 57–63.

13. In the article "Of Clouds and Clocks" (i.e. of soft, organic systems such as "real," naturally grown cities, on one hand; and of machines, computers, faxes, on the other) Karl Popper argues that the electronic and information era cannot escape the limitations of the machine age. We can call the early modernist "living machine" a hard system built primarily to minimize chance environmental influences. Through the growing electronic revolution the machine (clock type) evolved into a more complex system (computer type) with built-in relays and on/off switches that can "compensate" for "cloudlike" effects. Nonetheless the late modernist "living computer," argues Popper, remains essentially a means of control, from the inside out: control over the landscape, over society, over human behavior, over the spirit. Karl Popper, "Of Clouds and Clocks," in *Objective Knowledge—An Evolutionary Approach* (Oxford: Oxford University Press, 1972; rev. ed., 1986), 206–55.

14. Following Popper's critique in "Of Clouds and Clocks" (see note 13), the choice left to the spectator is only apparent, zapping from one channel to the other, and moreover, open to manipulation from above.

15. Le Corbusier, *Towards a New architecture*, 46.

16. See Bill Hillier and Julienne Hanson, *The Social Logic of Space* (Cambridge, Eng.: Cambridge University Press, 1984), 60, where the authors compare the preurban settlement to a "cloud of midges"; see also 42–45.

17. Ibid., 202: "Society is not a dance or a ritual, it is at the very least a statistical not a mechanical reality."

18. See Franz W. Kaiser, "Karel Appel: On Sensuality in Art," *Forum International* 6 (1991): 65:

> However, in the young painting of the eighties, which simultaneously countenances everything between geometrical abstraction and naturalistic representation, Neo-Informalism is conspicuously absent. Perhaps it has still to come, but perhaps Informalism was really a cul-de-sac after all. By contrast, Appel's work, which never took up a dogmatic stance towards the object or form, but always moved between different positions, is surprisingly modern again today.

19. Hillier and Hanson, *The Social Logic of Space*, 47.

20. Arthur I. Miller, "Gestalt Psychology and Genetic Epistemology," in *Imagery in Scientific Thought*, 281.

21. About propositions and prepositions, see Michel Foucault, *The Order of Things—An Archaeology of the Human Sciences* (London: Tavistock Publications, 1970), 99–100. Originally published in French under the title *Les Mots et les Choses* (Paris: Editions Gallimard, 1966).

22. Colin Rowe, "La Tourette," in *The Mathematics of the Ideal Villa and Other Essays* (Cambridge: MIT Press, 1976), 187.

23. The concept derives—via the chapel of Ronchamp, constructed out of seven bowed trapezia—from the serapeum of Villa Hadrianus in Tivoli, which is similarly constructed out of two rectangular planes. At Ronchamp the trapezium rule deforms according to the slope on which the chapel is built. Thus, an external factor determines Ronchamp's formal composition. See Martine De Maeseneer and Dirk Van den Brande, "How Exterior Planes Become Inside Ones: A Design Conception on the Chapel of Ronchamp," *Year Book H.A.I.S.L.G. 1991–92* (Ghent: Center for Architectural Research, 1993), 24–35.

24. Arthur Wortmann, "Culture/Architecture," *Grote Winkler Prins Jaarboek 1994* (Amsterdam: Bonaventura-Kluwer-Het Spectrum Editions, 1994), 322–23.

25. Glass as used in this context tackles the properties of immateriality, lack of memory ("meaning" or "figure" won't stick to glass), openness, light, and air associated with glass in the modern age.

26. However, on a more personal level, since he can choose to take either the front alley, passing by his new secretary—young, blond, and ornamental—or the back alley, passing by his wife—middle-aged and in control of the computers—the male owner is caught in a triangular relationship in which he is the uncertain element.

27. The combination of pinwheel structures, open/closed cellular clusters, and looplike corridors also appears in two postwar buildings designed by Le Corbusier. In his design for a hospital in Venice, the combination of pinwheel and looplike circulation distinguishes among several diseases and/or their treatments. From the center of the building, determined by a regulating diagram, a pinwheel of cells is removed, rotated and replaced, next to the building. This gives an insight into the composition of the building: the generative rule is placed outside and in front of the building. It also attempts to bridge the difference in scale between the large hospital and the finer grain of the surroundings (city of Venice). The second building is the monastery of La Tourette, which very much relates to the plan of the Venetian hospital despite the formal differences. Both buildings are constructed on the same regulating lines. In both the most public space is located in the center, demarcated by the regulating grid: in La Tourette, it is the meeting hall in front of the refectory, the only spot that allows for social contact. La Tourette therefore provides a variation on the theme of open/closed entirely located in the interfacial. "One is entitled to speak and to socialize in the meeting space, however in the corridors, refectory, church one remains quiet." See Anton Henze, *La Tourette—The LeCorbusier Monastery* (London: Percy Lund Humphries & Co., 1966).

28. It seems obvious to associate the overheating of the Newtonian machine (our general thesis) with the sexual impetus. Without going into the problems here, a hypothesis is offered by Jean-François Lyotard, who associates the matrix calculus, product of post-Newtonian physics and Werner Heisenberg's Uncertainty Principle, with the Freudian "unblocking" of unspeakable sexual traumas encountered in childhood. See Rosalind Krauss, "The Im/pulse to See," in *Vision and Visionality*, ed. Hal Foster (Seattle: Bay Press, 1988), 64–67.

29. At this point I offer a further explanation: in the first round of the competition each of the eight participants was commissioned to design both a small island (four houses) and a large island (eight houses). The design of the small island we chose to pass to the Chicago-based team of Linda Pollari and Robert Somol. The main theme of their project was to articulate the free section, in contrast to the modern free plan, which amounted to houses of three to four stories. The jury, obliged to choose between large and small island, and in effect between horizontally and vertically articulated projects, eventually chose the larger island. This inspired Somol to describe their design as "a monolithic and singular whole fallen apart after inspection." Our Sloten II project picks up these pieces again. See Bob Somol, "Real Abstract—Grift, Parole, and the Chicago Frame," in Martine de Maeseneer: *The In-di-visible Space*; reprinted in *Assemblage* 23 (April 1994): 70–85.

International School Complex, Lyon.
1989–92. (© Michel Dieudonne)

Chapter 3

A SIDE

I am not sure that I have any theoretical point of view about our practice.

All I know is that I am making things, I am building projects, I am doing my job the best I can. And also, in a way, I am honest with myself, with whom I am and with my general philosophical and political opinions.

It could be that the different points of view in the different projects contradict each other, but that is also very important: to admit that I might say "yes" one day, the day after say "yes but," and the day after say "no."

Exploiting Contradiction

I think that now, and ultimately since the beginning of this century, with the advent of information technology and mass media, previous codes or categories of people defined by locale are redundant. There are codes or categories of people who are, politically speaking, living together but not necessarily in the same place: we may be closer to somebody who is in Houston than to our neighbors. This has completely changed the topography of relationships between people. Any population may now consist of categories of people living together but independently from each other.

In buildings it is exactly the same: there are different networks of "things" in build-ings that each have their own life, their own logic, their own technology, and their own architecture, and that can be superimposed onto each other and still maintain their own logic.

This complexity (and the inherent mass of contradictions) has been quite new for us. For instance, we started out with the Lyon School of Architecture: here there is a very big contradiction between the upper level for the studios and the lower one for the classrooms: two logics, two geometries. We tried to find a general structure that could link the different geometries of the different orders. In fact, we tried to order the whole of existence, the whole world. Now we realize that this is no longer the issue, nor is it possible. We stopped that.

Lyon School of Architecture, Vaulx en Velin Initial analysis of the practice of architectural education clearly identified four types of teaching, distinguished by their capacity to encourage or hamper the student's personal expression and autonomy:

- the teaching of theoretical knowledge, adopting the conventional pedagogical relationship;
- experiments with theoretical knowledge where the student is not only receptive but responsive, individually or in a group;
- training in the process of project conception and design, where the student is relatively autonomous and personally responsible; and
- exhibition and public reviews enabling the acquisition of "parallel" knowledge and the possibility of confrontation with "others" (students, artists, architects, etc.).

This analysis resulted in the categorization of the different program elements into a series of teaching areas that manifest the various teacher/pupil relationships:

- theoretical teaching areas (classrooms, library, and laboratories) form the ground floor or base: a thick, heavy, megalithic, and compartmental structure;
- workshop and studio areas form the continuous space of the first floor or superstructure: a gossamer, light, transparent, and continuous structure;

and

- exhibition and review areas irrigate the entire length and height of the building, forming an interior street and square.

This strict dissociation of space articulates the legendary antagonism between the necessary acquisition of knowledge and indispensable, inevitable personal experimentation: between the Daedalean base and the airy superstructure whose wings recall Icarus's resistance.

However, here the base is not only a support for the workshop space above but also (and ironically) the necessary anchorage for the light, articulated structure. This stratification is split and revealed along the length of the building by the central street, a public space on the scale of the building.

The workshop superstructure, made with laminated wood beams connected by molded steel parts whose form directly derives from the analysis of forces they must transmit, forms an "attic" where the student develops his or her personal work. It is a fluid space simply punctuated by the rhythms of the structure, the stairs to the podia, and the giant vents. In the Daedalean base, the concrete arches are composed of prefabricated segments, dry constructed on curved wooden shuttering, the keystones on the diagonal arches being the only elements cast on site.

Aesthetics, Geometry, and Calculation

We have no aesthetic point of view regarding architecture. I am really unable to say "that is nice" or "that is beautiful and that is ugly." I am sure now that the only way to feel that something is beautiful is to know that it is true, and this truth (verité) or truthfulness (veracité) can only be right if we allow the design process to reach that point, if we are very honest, if we accept everything.

This is why we find ourselves working with highly complex geometries: it is not an aim in itself but the natural consequence of the projects. Geometry, as an external imposed order, would become in this condition something very arbitrary. It might serve as a way of reassuring ourselves about a reality, but ultimately it would be something completely wrong.

In some of our more recent projects the spaces are so complex that they must be calculated, not drawn. Today we are able to calculate and model this complexity via computer. This new power of calculation allows us more freedom, knowing that ostensibly everything is possible. In the past, spaces needed to be simplified in order to be drawn. Twenty or

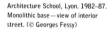

Architecture School, Lyon. 1982–87. Monolithic base — view of interior street. (© Georges Fessy)

thirty years ago this simple inability to solve geometric problems was hidden behind an aesthetic conversation about order and symmetry and the idea of a "nice" drawing. Aesthetics provided a pretext, a political pretext. It was a good pretext not to ask the right questions about architecture because the tools were not there. Now the tools are available, and it is no longer possible to avoid asking certain questions.

For us, for instance, there is no sense in making a façade.

International School Complex, Lyon The International School is a sort of giant question mark stretched out along the edge of the Rhône, with the communal spaces (the "village") nestling into its curve, protected by a tensile canopy planted with grass.

Facing the confluence of the Rhône and Saône, the linear classroom building slopes gently from seven to three levels towards the south, as it slides from the older students to the younger. The river facade to the west is entirely glazed, behind which are placed, in a slot seven meters high and three hundred meters long, stairways, footbridges, podiums, technical blocks, and interior gardens. In the summer this temperate area is left open. On the other face, the classrooms look out over a planted roof through the glazed east and south walls of the building, which are protected by ribbons of motorized aluminum awnings that track the sun throughout the day.

The village, composed of quadrilateral boxes that jostle for position beneath this freely twisting field, is traversed like the Lyon School of Architecture by an interior street. Here one finds all spaces common to the three schools (primary, intermediate and upper). These collective spaces (library, game room, canteen, annexes to the gymnasiums, conference areas, and laboratories) are enclosed concrete and wooden structures. Between them and also protected by the roof are the "exterior" yet sheltered public spaces of the village: interior street, terraces, gymnasium.

The grass roof protecting these buildings measures 8,000 square meters and is hung at a height varying from four to twelve meters above the ground floor. It is cut out of an eight-meter-square grid of beams to form a blanket that has been deformed, lifted, and twisted at each of the intersections to obtain the desired height at each point. This operation results in a roof in motion, with a chaotic or "humpy" appearance, lacking any architectural aesthetic or

International School Complex. Aerial view. (Jourda & Perraudin)

preconceptions with regard to the overall geometry. Similarly, the masts are simply tilted to sit perpendicular to the tangent of the roof's approximated curve at the point of intersection.

The roof surface is made of ribbed steel sheeting, forming a double curved surface that carries waterproofing, drainage, and a layer for the vegetation. A strip over the interior street is glazed by eight hundred sheets of glass of variously angled trapezoidal panes, each slightly different in shape, bolted together and sealed with silicon to create a strange transparent armor. This complex surface was plotted by computer. The specific angle of each sheet was calculated (not drawn); each sheet received special spiderlike fixings that could adjust to carry it in its own plane before being bolted onto the structure. Underneath this seething roof, the village maintains its own internal logic.

International School. View of interior
street. (© Georges Fessy)

Practicing Complexity

One consequence of using the computer's calculation power to build more complex geometries is that we are not able to anticipate every space in a design. For instance, when the underground space (the village) in the International School Complex in Lyon was on site we were literally discovering it as it was being built.

It was very important for us to just accept the idea of not having everything in our brains, and it was very difficult because we felt guilty for not being able to do that. Then we decided that we couldn't. We decided to admit that things had to be built without our agreement. So the work became not how to find the solution but how to find the rules for finding the solution—not to design the points where the connections between the different geometries and logics cross but to design the different rules needed to solve these points.

This was a great change in our practice; the problems are now solved as the building is built, and it works because it follows the rules. This is what makes the solution "right."

In theory we can superimpose as many codes as we need, but in reality, for technical and economic reasons, that is not possible. So we decided to establish an erasure process, to take out some layers or codes where these codes had no influence on the space and the quality of the space. Erasure became the point of intervention. With the exactitude of the computer we could superimpose the different layers, but then with the need to erase we would come in and work over this structure, move different things. It was about necessity; very often it is the only way of working, just to accept the necessity of a thing.

This theoretical complexity has changed our way of approaching projects and of representing projects during the design process: interior perspectives are now of no use because the geometry is so complex that a single view of one part from a certain position is irrelevant; the viewer need take only one step to the side and the view changes. Spatial complexity requires multiple systems of representation including ones that incorporate movement.

This can be achieved via computerized walk-through perspectives; however, in practice there is never the money to buy the computer time necessary, to study the project to this depth. We always have to hurry to prepare the next stage. So again all we can do is make sure that the concept of the geometry is good enough, that it can accept the different variations and events in the building.

When you first skim the surface of a new project, the complexity is not there; at the beginning, only part of the information reveals itself. We may try to resolve a building with only three categories of data, but as we gather more and more information and have more contact with the client and the client changes his mind (and continues to change his mind every two days), the reality, the life of the project emerges. Then we have more and more information, *more and more changes demanding more and more deformations of the project; and then it starts to become complex. We try to find new tools as we go. The projects have never yet reached saturation point, but it may happen.*

Signal Building for the University of Marne la Vallée As the name implies, the signal building acts as a beacon for the whole university complex and also houses a collection of auditoriums in its base and an open restaurant and cafe above. Its architecture takes advantage of the implicit contradiction in the program (lecturing and catering) by referring to two strategies—inclusion and the "atmospheric roof"—and exploiting the necessary cohabitation of the two systems.

Abandoning any preconceptions with regard to the composition of the space, we were able to adopt an inclusive approach allowing the autonomy of each strategy despite its necessary coexistence with the other. Consequently, the building accommodates and embodies two conflicting desires:

Signal building for University of Marne
la Vallée. 1992–95.

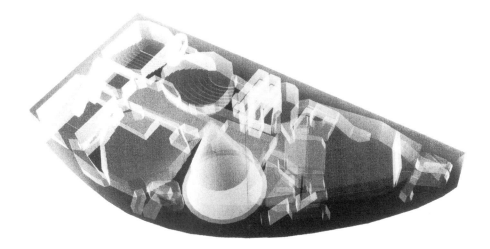

- the desire to satisfy the external view and to comply with the urban logic of a compact building
- the desire to satisfy the internal view, or rather multiple views, and to allow multiple architectures to express themselves individually

Similarly, the atmospheric roof proposes the systematic superposition of various climatic, luminous, acoustic, and service systems, negotiating places where they collide (via erasure) and exploiting these points of interference

On the Envelope

If geometry is understood as consequential, the facade becomes a quite different animal, part of a wraparound envelope. A thickness. A totally artificial interruption between interior and exterior that negotiates between architecture and the environment.

With building technology, and especially with the mechanical technology now available (heating, climatic, ventilation, etc.), there is a real danger of using the facade as something abstract that divides indoors from outdoors, comfortable climate from something dangerous (too hot or too cold). Always protecting the people inside the building. I have problems with "comfort" with no buffer zone, no intermediary space between indoors and outdoors. It is not good for our health, it is very expensive in energy terms; but more than that, politically, it means that people are always trying to have the best conditions in their buildings, and what goes on outdoors doesn't matter.

Ultimately the place where people can still meet, where people can be together, can see others, is outside. How they discover the outdoor world is very important. The facade can't simply be a piece of glass; it must be a filter, a screen. It must appropriate the outside world to bring it inside, and not always by softening it: as with the atmospheric roof in the University of Marne la Vallée building, we can choose to amplify certain conditions.

These may be social as well as climatic conditions, and the occupants may appropriate the envelope to their own devices. If a woman does not like somebody, she just turns her head not to see him; so should a building allow the possibility of not having to always confront external conditions. But these conditions themselves can change, so we must be able to change the relationships, the skin, the different screens through which we see the environment—by which I mean the social or climatic environment or just a landscape or noise.

It is a question of allowing the different screens or filters of the building to make up a responsive skin, part of a search for an envelope that can respond to its environment in a

symbiotic relationship between landscape and architecture. Ultimately we anticipate a skin that can respond to the extremes of climate, pollution, future atmospheres: a sort of living matter that will open or close as the need arises. Not protection, but active, enervated tissue. Responsive architecture is an architecture sensitive to nature and to man-made surroundings, definitively closed off but still interactive, almost evolving, no longer schizophrenic.

This refers to what I call the schizophrenia between indoors and outdoors, and it applies to people too. Some people are divided in two parts, one works, and one lives with the family. My response is always the same very personal point of view: we cannot have two heads and two faces. I am just one person. We must acknowledge the need not to change ourselves in different environments but to change the environments. If we are not comfortable in one place, we should go somewhere else. This has not been possible in the past because of material difficulties, but now it is easier; for instance, it is now possible within a building to transport information via cable. So why should we live as in the Middle Ages, having a life-long place to work and live? Buildings should be able to move and transport themselves, and people should move with them and within them. That means that people must be able to accept the movement, the change of environment. That is most difficult for people who desire fixity, who feel secure when they are somewhere and when they stay there and they think that they will stay there all their lives. They know what that space is for.

The appealing notion of the transparent facade or envelope is a delusion, for there is no real transparency. In addition, this transparency, this notion of a skin as a sheet of glass, far from creating a harmonious relationship with the environment (on the pretext of having the interior and the exterior "communicate"), creates an artificial interruption, establishing within a few millimeters an invisible yet insurmountable barrier. But what if the interior spaces are allowed to appropriate, to take possession of the envelope, and the envelope is allowed to amplify certain external conditions?

The Atmospheric Roof (Signal Building for the University of Marne la Vallée) The atmospheric roof is not merely intended to confirm the external conditions or atmosphere within the limits of a minimum comfort—which would flatten the curve of the spatial emotions—but also to amplify exterior phenomena and to transform them in order to render perceptible environmental changes within the buildings. Various systems are deployed, such as "spores" or leaves on the glass roof that will move in the breeze, reflecting the sun into the building, creating mobile light effects. The roof will conduct natural light into the heart of the building and also respond to the wind speed and direction, ambi-

ent temperature, and visibility so as to animate the internal environment of
numbed comfort.

The Temporal

*Buildings should respond to outdoor conditions. They should be able to transform their own
clothes, their own different skins, to open them up or to change them. We should also imagine
a building as something that will not necessarily remain for two centuries but might disappear, be transformed—very different from the lasting architecture of the past, very conscious
of its own and next destruction.*

*Our house was designed for people with young children. Our children are getting
older; we will have to transform our house, to destroy it and build something new.*

*We must also be very careful using energy and natural resources. Perhaps we should
think about a light architecture. But lightness does not only mean transparency; it also
means that we have less material and less weight, but it can be very deep. For instance, in
Marne la Vallée on the ground floor, where all the lecture halls are, we used very deep walls
(five- or six-meter diaphragm construction), but there is only void between the two skins.
In the next ten or twenty-five years they will find a use for that space; why should we solve
everything and decide everything for the future now?*

House, Lyon-Vaise Our house, like the International School Complex in Lyon,
is sheltered underneath an independent blanket: as man under a tent or prehis-
toric man under foliage. It is a way of referring to the way one is sited, to the
sense of being both an object of a certain a scale while still inventing new
boundaries, new forms. The house design reinterprets daily existence as it
directly relates to certain fundamental physical conditions: water, earth, day,
night.

The house stands in an orchard of a presbytery on a site enclosed by
high walls. In order to preserve the existing vegetation, the house is supported
on a number of points and thus "floats" above the ground. The main structure
is steel; the cladding, wood and glass. Entirely prefabricated, it was erected in
only a few days. The roof, an artificial canopy and an extension of the neigh-
boring plane trees, was hung in one day and provided effective shelter for the
rest of the construction site.

The actual habitat is a plywood box: two layers of plywood on wooden
stiffeners enclosing thermal insulation. The same material is used for ceilings,

Signal building for University of Marne
la Vallée. Three layers of the atmospheric roof. (Jourda & Perraudin)

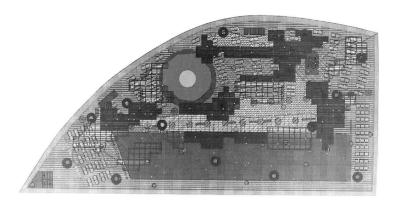

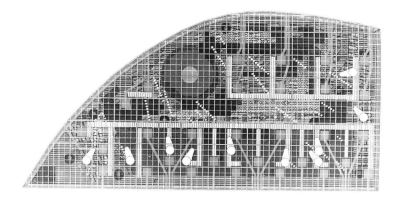

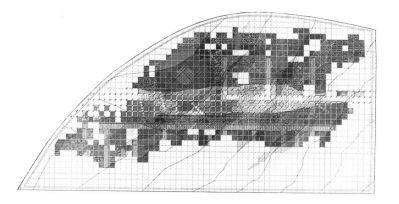

floors, and partitions. The east, west, and north sides are completely opaque while the southern facade is made entirely of sliding glass doors, establishing physical and visual continuity between the dwelling and the garden. Wide terraces sheltered by the roof extend to form outdoor living rooms. The play of openings and closures of the facade panels allow the house to breathe and are complemented by blinds to control the luminosity and the growth cycles of interior vegetation.

The Oneiric

Our idea is that we must accept reality; however, this does not mean that we must only be pragmatic. We must accept the whole reality, the spirit of things, what is lurking in the imagination of Lyon, the world of fantasy.

Because we have no aesthetic direction, there are two possibilities. One is just to gather enough information to explore and generate a space from these different codes or data brought together. But sometimes the information is not available—or not relevant—and this leads to the other solution: a "modern design," very pure and smooth and simple.

House at Lyon Vaise. 1987. (© Haüser)

But we are not able to do that, I mean, we are able but we are not interested in doing that. The other possibility is a kind of aesthetic alternative: if you have no aesthetic agenda, then a design can go in any direction. We might say, "Well, let's just express the dream of these objects, the fantasy attached to that thing or situation." It is difficult for a designer to work with this freedom. To say, "Let's have leaves here or a dragon or a pig's head there," to accept it and admit it as a possibility. Perhaps especially for me it is very difficult.

Metro Projects Lyon The spirit of a city lies neither in its functionality nor in its technicality. It lies in its history, its secrets, its territory, its geography. The history of Lyon ferments in the underground, in its galleries and passageways. It has been ripening for centuries, creating a concentrated energy that emerges from time to time. In Lyon, the ground is not stable. It is a fragile boundary between the underground world and the aerial world, the sacred and the profane.

The canopies for Metro line D testify via their imagery to an underground life, to dragons springing up out of the earth to signal the entrances of the main stations on this line. They seek both to provoke and promote this form of public transport, acting as sign, shelter, and information point. The spine is a cast aluminum shell, sandblasted and coated with an antigraffiti medium; the translucent sections or webs mounted onto the articulated limbs are polycarbonate.

The Parilly metro station is situated in a barely urbanized part of the suburbs, at the crossing of several main roads. In this architecture of the underground, dug out of the mass, daylight penetrates by means of two voids in the building's main hall. The design exploits the plasticity of the concrete and the line of force of the arcs borne by the slanted lateral columns. The mixture of two geometries (the 5.4-square-meter grid and the seventy-one-degree angle of the rails in relation to the grid) led to a structure of arches and crossed vaults made of exposed concrete, according to a geometry that optimizes forces transmitted from the upper slab (the ground floor of the building above) to the ground below. Each of the elements (shafts, chapters, arches, and vaults) was designed in direct relation to the construction techniques employed (metal shuttering, on-site concrete casting, prefabricated vaults). Thus the architecture is in perfect accord with matter.

Materiality

The idea of immaterial architecture, very current in France at least, is something I cannot really understand because I think that the material and the physical are increasingly important. We are always working with virtual things; computers are a virtual world, something that does not exist, something that you can't touch or feel. You can't tell if it's cold or hot; there is no temperature, there is no, well, nothing. Because of this we need things material. For instance, we work with computers and also with lots of models. We must find a balance between the two, and for architecture I think it is exactly the same thing, we must keep remembering we are people who need to be protected, by things, by clothes. We must keep this aspect of reality in our minds. We are quite fragile.

Maisons Pisées, l'Isle d'Abeau The extraordinary specificity of *pisé* (packed clay) brought a set of directive constraints to this housing project on the Isle d'Abeau: the strength only in compression, the absolute need for protection from water, and the fact that it can only go on site in the spring or summer because of its slow setting.

The dwellings were divided into two groups formed by massive blocks of earth raised off the ground on a cement foundation. Each block is a duplex on three levels and is protected and seasonably attenuated by the overlapping and continuous glass roof and a series of awnings, trellises, and screen walls forming multiple envelopes as in a Russian doll.

Second (Upstream) Austerlitz Bridge Spanning 120 meters, the form and the geometry of this shell-structure bridge directly derive from the constraints with which it must comply: vehicular and pedestrian traffic are considered as fluids, and the shape of the bridge emerged from the curves that facilitate their flow. Matter is precisely arranged to achieve the equitable distribution of forces throughout the entire structure. The structure itself, which compares to the porous structure of bone, is composed of fine interlaced membranes; on a larger scale, it forms a homogeneous material. With the help of computer programs hitherto used in the nuclear industry, the structure's geometry and the thickness of the membranes can be adapted, almost interactively, to structural constraints.

The resulting shapes are close to natural forms; the construction techniques—such as the automated plasma cutting of the steel sheets—are bor-

Maison en Pisé, L'Isle d'Abeau. 1981–85. (Jourda & Perraudin)

rowed from shipbuilding. The envelope is made of composite sheets of stainless and carbon steel, with the stainless steel side turned outward on all visible facings; the envelope contributes to the structure's integrity.

I try to make projects just like I am. We all think, eat, drink, and make love. We must accept this.

This is not a theoretical statement. It is just different points of view. I have opinions about everything, but they may diverge—it is not something very continuous, there may be contradictions, but I have no time to solve them. That is not my objective.

Part of the skeleton of a siliceous
sponge fossil and computer studies of
the ends of the new Austerlitz bridge
showing the shell structure, Paris.
1988. (Jourda & Perraudin)

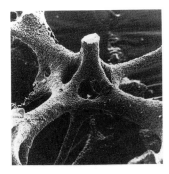

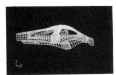

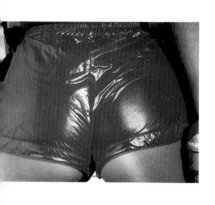

Chapter 4   **B** AD **P** RESS   Elizabeth Diller

Private Property

To identify what falls under the category of indecent public exposure for recent antinudity legislation, the state of Florida produced a legal definition of the human buttocks:

Extract: The area at the rear of the human body which lies between two imaginary lines running parallel to the ground when a person is standing—the first or top of such line drawn at the top of the cleavage of the nates (i.e. the prominence formed by the muscles running from the back of the hip to the back of the leg) and the second or bottom line drawn at the lowest visible point of this cleavage or the lowest point of the curvature of the fleshy protuberance, whichever is lower, and—between two imaginary lines on each side of the body, which run perpendicular to the ground and to the horizontal lines described above, and which perpendicular lines are drawn through the point at which each nate meets the outer side of each leg.[1]

Any exposure of flesh within this rectangular boundary would constitute a legal infraction. Unlike land law, where property lines protect the space of the private from transgressions of the public, the property lines that define the socially "decent" body defend public space from transgressions of the private(s). The play between *property* and *propriety* or the *proper*[2] is particularly intricate in considering the body as a legal site.

But the body has long been a site of uncertain jurisdiction, from Kafka's harrowing inscription of the crime against the state onto the body of the accused to William Buckley's proposal to legally mandate that all homosexuals testing HIV positive have their buttocks tattooed. More common are invisible markings onto social bodies—for example, the bodies produced by disciplinary technologies and techniques of power discussed by Michel Foucault. Here the body is inseparable from the institutional structure, as is the body of the soldier, "instrumentally coded at the most minute levels. The articulation of his every gesture, from his marching posture to his penmanship was broken down into its component parts, each of which was assigned a duration and an order of appearance"[3] and invested with as much representational value as the uniform covering his skin. But bodies, as we know, are constructed by subtler mechanisms of control—like the fashionable body produced by popular media. This body is continually being reinscribed by a complex weave of discourses including health, beauty, economy, and geography.

Homebodies

At the end of the nineteenth century, the body began to be understood as a mechanical component of industrial productivity, an extension of the factory apparatus. Scientific management, or Taylorism, sought to rationalize and standardize the motions of this body, harnessing its dynamic energy and converting it to efficient labor power. According to Anson Rabinbach, "the dynamic language of energy was central to many utopian social and political ideologies of the early twentieth century: Taylorism, Bolshevism, and fascism. All of these movements viewed the body both as a productive force and as a political instrument whose energies could be subjected to scientifically designed systems of organization."[4]

It was not long before the practice of engineering bodies for the factory was introduced into the office, the school, and the hospital. By the first decade of the twentieth century, scientific management was brought into the home and applied to domestic housework. Time-motion studies developed to dissect every action of the factory laborer, with the intention of designing ideal shapes of movement and, ultimately, the ideal laborer, were imported into the home to scrutinize every movement exerted in housekeeping in order to produce the ideal housewife. (The term *housewife*, which had been in use since the thirteenth

century in Europe, required reconceptualizing both "wife" and "house" in relation to the servantless, middle-class American household of the 1920s). Scientific management interpreted the body of this housewife as a dynamic force with unlimited capacity for work. Her only enemy was fatigue, and fatigue, in broader terms, undermined the moral imperative of the new social reform—the reclamation of all waste as usable potential.

When Frank Gilbreth raised the efficiency of bricklaying by reducing stooping, Christine Frederick, the earliest exponent of scientific efficiency in the home, asked "Didn't I with hundreds of women stoop unnecessarily over kitchen tables, sinks and ironing boards, as bricklayers stoop over bricks?"

Two excerpts from the 1950s and 1960s:

Extract: Pre-cooked foods, made possible by new packaging developments, are a major time-saver for housewives. Notice the difference in time and effort required in the preparation of a pre-cooked, pre-packaged goulash dinner and one fixed entirely from scratch. Lights attached to the cook's wrists show how many more movements she had to make in the 90 minutes it took the long way, compared with the pre-cooked way which took only 12 minutes.[5]

Reaching with the arms to heights of 46″, 56″, and 72″ above the floor, requires an increase of oxygen consumed per minute over simply standing of 12%, 24%, and 50%, respectively. The energy consumed is therefore in proportion to the height of the reach. Reaching up with the arms takes less energy than bending the body. Reaching by means of a trunk bend to 22″ and to 3″ above the floor, increases oxygen consumption above that required for standing to 57% and 131% of cubic centimeters of oxygen per minute. Reaching by using a knee bend to 3″ above the floor, requires 224% oxygen consumption. While this would indicate that a trunk bend requires less energy than a knee bend, the knee bend is believed to involve less muscular strain.[6]

The application of labor-saving techniques from scientific management, in conjunction with the introduction of household appliances, the new "electric servants," sought to conserve the physical expenditure of the 1920s housewife. The time and energy saved, according to the rhetoric of efficiency, would release the woman from the home and thus enable her to join the paid labor force.

The drive for efficiency, however, did not fulfill its liberating promise. Efficiency was often taken as an objective in itself. Ironically, it condemned the housewife to an increased workload as the expectations and standards of cleanliness in the home rose to compulsive levels. The discovery of the "household germ" and the proliferation of germ theory galvanized a link between dirt and disease. Dirt soon became a moral construct yielding sexual, religious, and aesthetic distinctions. The fetishization of hygiene blurred the problem of cleanliness with beauty, chastity, piety, and modernity. As efficiency targeted domestic space as much as the domestic body, the design of the interior succumbed to this paranoid hygiene. The dust and germ-breeding intricacies of the nineteenth-century interior collapsed into pure surface—white, smooth, flat, nonporous, and seamless—under the continuous disciplinary watch of the housewife.

Although the application of scientific management to housework did not liberate the housewife, daily work in the home became increasingly rationalized by the women condemned to stay there. In order to remove the stigma from what was considered to be the service-oriented menial labor of the female, daily housework between the 1920s and 1940s was progressively masculinized and reconfigured into a more comprehensive economic management of the household.[7] The "home economist" now combined the skills of nutritionist, doctor, accountant, child-care specialist, and informed consumer, among others.

Notwithstanding this new characterization, the actual physical labor involved in housework remained just as demanding and distasteful as it had ever been. The dirt previously absorbed by the body of the servant was now a direct concern to the woman of the house.[8] In the servantless household of the first half of the century, the maintenance of the idealized female body that exhibited no evidence of decay became a project of devotion equal to that of the maintenance of idealized domestic space. Both were dedicated to preventing the corrosions of age and to the daily restoration of an ideal order whose standards and values were produced and sustained in the popular media.

Today, home and body maintenance have found a new conjunction: household chores can be incorporated into a daily aerobic regimen and performed to the beat of a television fitness trainer. No longer socially isolated, the maintainer of the home can perform household tasks with countless other viewers. Even though housework is slowly becoming less gendered and the discrete sites of "work" and "leisure" exchangeable, most conventions of domestic maintenance remain unchallenged. Housework's primary activities of managing dirt and restoring daily order continue to be subjected to the economic ethos of industry, guided by motion-economy principles originally designed by efficiency engineers. Take, for example, the procedure for ironing a man's shirt outlined by a 1960s housekeeping manual:

Extract: Center the back of the shirt on an ironing board with the yoke taut. Lifting the iron as little as possible, draw the iron, with its point facing the collar down the yoke to the rear tail hem and press the box pleat, using unhurried, well-directed, rhythmic motions. To avoid unnecessary manipulation of the garment, rotate the shirt in the following sequence: first, counterclockwise over the ironing surface to expose the left front panel. Press. Pause when pressing each button hole and pocket, allowing the steam to penetrate the fabric facing and inner band. Next, rotate the shirt clockwise to expose the right front panel and press, rotating the tip of the iron around every button. Slide the right shoulder yoke over the tip of the ironing board and press. Repeat with the left shoulder yoke. Lay out the right sleeve with the placket facing up and iron diagonally across the sleeve width from the underarm seam joint to the upper edge of the sleeve cuff, pressing in a sharp crease. Repeat this procedure for the left sleeve. With the rear yoke centered, press the undercollar and collar crease, working the sole plate toward the collar tips. Turn the shirt over with its front facing up and fasten the buttons. Using the Z-method to eliminate unnecessary

movements of garment and arms, turn the shirt over. Fold the left rear facet in, toward the center, pressing in a sharp crease from the outer edge of the yoke shoulder, 2 1/2 inches out from the undercollar seam to the tail hem. Fold the left sleeve 45 degrees at the shoulder seam so that the length of the sleeve runs parallel along the length of the rear facet crease and press. Repeat this procedure for the right rear facet and right sleeve. Fold the shirt tail 1/3 of the way toward the collar. Fold 1/3 over again to the yoke, ensuring that all edges are aligned and form ninety degree corners. Using the Z-method, turn the shirt over with its front facing out and press lightly.

With the advent of the electric iron, the task of ironing became progressively governed by minimums, both aesthetic and economic. A minimum of effort is

used to reshape the shirt through a minimum of flat facets into a two-dimensional, repetitive unit that will consume a minimum of space. This shirt will exhibit a minimum of creases when worn, particularly in the exposed area between the lapels of the jacket. The standardized ironing pattern of a man's shirt habitually returns the shirt to a flat, rectangular shape that fits economically into orthogonal storage systems—at the site of manufacture, the factory-pressed shirt is stacked and packed into rectangular cartons that are loaded as cubic volumes onto trucks and transported to retail space where the shirt's rectangular form is reinforced in orthogonal display cases and then, after purchase, sustained in the home on closet shelves or in dresser drawers, and finally, on trips away from home, in suitcases. The shirt is disciplined at every stage to conform to an unspoken social contract.

Shirt 1

When worn, the residue of the orthogonal logic of efficiency is registered on the surface of the body. The parallel creases and crisp, square corners of a clean, pressed shirt have become sought after emblems of refinement. The by-product of efficiency has become a new object of its desire.

But what if the task of ironing were to free itself from the aesthetics of efficiency altogether? Perhaps the effects of ironing could more aptly represent the postindustrial body by trading the image of the functional for that of the dysfunctional.

Bad Press

(Instructions for a dissident ironing)

Shirt 1: With the left front panel of the shirt over the ironing surface, pull the iron tip from the outer edge of the shoulder seam in a straight diagonal line down to

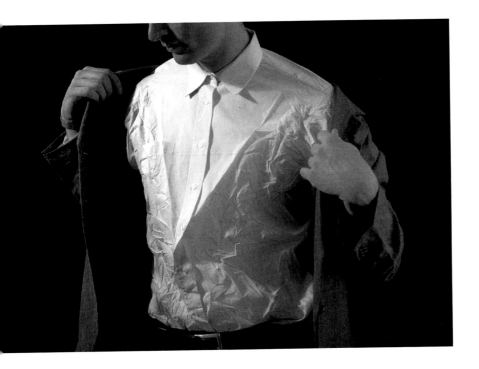

the fifth or sixth buttonhole, depending on the inner lapel angle of the jacket to be worn. Repeat this procedure for the right panel and press only the area inside the *V*. Press the collar crease, working the sole plate toward the front collar tips. Press the exposed two inches of the shirt cuffs only. Button the front and lightly press a sharp crease into the left and right *V* edges.

(*The English dandies of the eighteenth and nineteenth centuries introduced the conception of
personal cleanliness. The white shirt was introduced as a washable, socially accepted layer of
covering between underwear and outerwear. It represented a new sanitary order. Beau Brummel
is said to be responsible for the startling innovation of wearing a clean shirt daily.*)

Extract: According to the social gentility of dandyism, the white layer covering
the skin always extended beyond the edges of the overgarment at the wrists
and neck, serving as a sanitary frame for the obsessively well-groomed hands
and head. The detachable collar and cuffs were thus subjected to the most rigorous
boiling, starching, ironing and polishing. What was initially meant to
represent the new austerity in dress for the man, 'The Great Masculine Renunciation,'
turned into a fascination with artifice which transformed the image of
sobriety into the image of flamboyant efficiency.[9]

Shirt 2: Press the shirt according to ironing procedure but do not fold. With the
shirt facing up, fasten the second button into the first buttonhole at the collar.
Continue fastening the buttons in sequence, skipping the fourth buttonhole. The
remaining buttons will fall into alignment. Turn the shirt over and press the left
and right facets. Adjust for material discrepancy by skewing the shoulder ridge
and mid-fold to seven degrees from the horizontal median.

(*Prisoners assigned laundering detail in a state correctional facility have invented a highly
developed language articulated through the practice of ironing. Seemingly superfluous, decorative
creases pressed into the clothing of other prisoners are invested with representational
value understood only to the participants. Like the prison tattoo, another form of inscription
on soft, pliable surfaces, the crease is a mark of resistance by the marginalized. Where the
tattoo acts on the only possession left to the prisoner, the skin, the crease acts directly on
the institutional skin of the prison uniform—a camouflaged defacing. The crease resists
appropriation more so than the tattoo in that its abstract language is illegible to the uninitiated
compared with the typically pictorial language of the tattoo.*)

Shirt 3: Press the shirt flat. Keeping the back panel facing up, use standard ironing procedure, folding the right sleeve over the right facet. Keep the left sleeve free. Continue to press, folding the shirt along the axis of the right sleeve to reduce the shirt to the precise width of the front pocket. Fold the collar forward at a forty-five-degree angle to the shirt. Fold the right sleeve in half along its length and press. Cross-fold and bring the right sleeve up through the collar and, with a crease five inches from the cuff, tuck down into the pocket.

Shirt 2

Extract: When patient 'X' began ironing an article of clothing, she could not stop until she collapsed from exhaustion. The patient would meticulously, and without pause, press out the most imperceptible wrinkles in a shirt, for example, repeating the same areas over and over again. The wrinkles could never be completely removed, thus the job could never be properly finished according to her expectations—as new wrinkles would inevitably be introduced into the garment by the task of ironing itself.[10]

Shirt 4: Press the shirt without folding. Button the cuffs and front panels of the shirt. Push the collar into the shirt from the top and pull it out between the fourth and fifth buttons. Fold the cuffs back on themselves and iron flat. Pull the cuffs

Shirt 3

through the collar, keeping the crease axis at forty-five degrees. Fold the collar over and down. Press the left and right facets and press perpendicular folds before the third button and after the sixth.

Extract: Manufacturers are hailing the Japanese invention of a non-shrinking, durable press all-cotton shirt as the best new wrinkle in men's wear since the advent of permanent press shirts nearly three decades ago. Shirts represent the ultimate no-iron challenge because they are made of thin fabric compared with most other clothes. When cotton is worn and washed, the hydrogen bridges that connect the cellulose molecules in cotton can break. If bridges break, the molecular chains swell and shift upon washing and wrinkles form. However, when cotton is treated with resins and other reactive molecules, new bridges

Shirt 4

are formed between cotton molecules which stabilize the fabric. Shirt scientists, as it turns out, have a scale for classifying wrinkles, with 1.0 being the equivalent of a withered prune and 5.0 being ideal. The new shirts have a rating between 3.5 and 4.0. In Japan, where domestic chores are still divided largely along traditional gender lines, the shirts are proving popular not only with housewives who hate to iron, but also with salary men, who on business trips can now wash a shirt in the sink, hang it up to dry and wear it the next day.[11]

Certainly the popularity of permanent press miracle fabrics among Japanese businessmen is maintaining the image of labor expended by their wives.

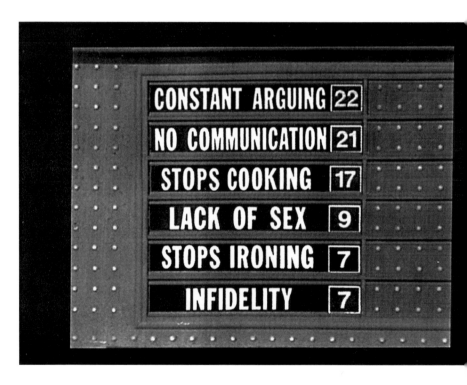

From the popular game show *Family Feud*: Master of Ceremonies: "Listen carefully to this question. We asked one hundred married men, 'Name one of the first warning signs that a marriage is going on the rocks.' The top six answers are on the board."

(*Perhaps with the advent of miracle fabrics, ironing will continue to linger as an expression of affection.*)

Shirt 5: Press the right sleeve with a crisp crease down the center. Turn the left sleeve inside-out. Press and pull the sleeve through the buttoned collar. Extend

Shirt 5

one hand through the inside of the right sleeve at placket end and grasp the shirt bottom at the front bands. Gather the shirt completely into the right sleeve until the collar meets the underarm seam. Align the collar and cuff with the vertical crease of the sleeve.

Two speculations on the Deleuzian fold:

Extract: John Rajchman: One cannot say that the 'fold' or 'pli,' is traditional to philosophy, though etymologically it is parent to many fold-words, words with -plic and -plex, like explication, implication, multiplicity and, perplexity, complexity or perplication and complication. The fold involves an 'affective' space. The modernist 'machines for living' sought to express a clean, efficient space for the new mechanical body; but who will invent a way to express the affective space for the new multiplicitous body?[12]

Greg Lynn: Culinary theory has developed a definition for three types of mixtures. The first involves the manipulation of homogeneous elements. Beating, whisking and whipping change the volume but not the nature of a liquid through agitation. The second mixes two or more disparate elements. Chopping, dicing, grinding, grating, slicing, shredding and mincing eviscerate elements into fragments. The third, folding, creaming and blending mix smoothly multiple ingredients through repeated gentle overturnings in such a way that their individual characteristics are maintained. If there is a single effect produced in architecture by folding, it will be the ability to integrate unrelated elements within a new continuous mixture. A folded mixture is neither homogeneous like whipped cream, nor fragmented like chopped nuts, but smooth and heterogeneous.[13]

Shirt 6: Turn the shirt inside-out and center on the ironing surface pulling plackets taut. Evenly divide the back panel length into twenty sections. Fold each section over accordion fashion and firmly press. With the entire shirt back folded and pressed, roll it back into the collar, leaving left and right front panels extending from the collar tips. Fold the collar over compressed shirt back and fasten the collar buttons. Reverse the inside-out sleeves over remaining side panels. Fasten the cuffs and press.

(*The fold has been a useful metaphor for the discourse of poststructuralist architecture, because it consolidates ambiguities, such as surface and structure, figure and organization. One of the prime attributes of the fold is that it is nonrepresentational. The fold also implies reversibility—if something can be folded, it can be unfolded and refolded.*)

(*The crease is a more compelling metaphor because it presents a resistance to transformation. The crease has a longer memory than the fold and it has representational value, in the nature of an inscription. The crease is harder to get out. Its traces guide their continual confirmation—until a new order is inscribed, with the illusion of permanence.*)

Shirt 6

Project assistants: Brendan Cotter, Heather Champ and John Bachus, Linda Chung, Paul Lewis, David Lindberg

Notes

1. Steve Marshall, "Bottom Line on Buttocks," *USA Today*, March 19, 1992.

2. This assemblage has been eloquently presented by Catherine Ingraham in "The Faults of Architecture: Troping the Proper," *Assemblage* 7 (1988): 7–13.

3. Robert McAnulty, "Body Troubles," in *Strategies in Architectural Thinking* (Cambridge: MIT Press, 1992).

4. Anson Rabinbach, *The Human Motor* (Berkeley: University of California Press, 1992).

5. Hazel Thompson, *Thresholds to Adult Living* (1955).

6. Esther Bratton, *Oxygen Consumed in Household Tasks*, Bulletin 873 (Ithaca: New York State College of Home Economics at Cornell University, 1952).

7. Paraphrased from Phyllis Palmer, *Domesticity and Dirt: Housewives and Domestic Servants in the United States, 1920–1945* (Philadelphia: Temple University Press, 1984).

8. Ibid.

9. Paraphrased from Zvi Effrat, "The Unseemliness of the Fashionable," *Architecture: In Fashion* (New York: Princeton Architectural Press, 1994).

10. Case citing schoolteacher under treatment for obsessional-compulsive disorder in the *Journal of Behavioral Research*.

11. "Low Iron 100% Cotton shirts Expected in the US by Father's Day," *New York Times*, December 30, 1993.

12. Paraphrased from John Rajchman, "Out of the Fold," *Architectural Design*, no. 102 "Folding in Architecture" (1993): 61–63.

13. Greg Lynn, "Architectural Curvilinearity," *Architectural Design*, no. 102 "Folding in Architecture" (1993): 9.

The I
tion of arch
but by their

actice

ation is arcl

and

Chapter 5

A PRACTICE OF ONE'S OWN: THE CRITICAL COPY AND TRANSLATION OF SPACE

Dagmar Richter

Architectural design as it is practiced every day is generally confined within the boundaries of representation. Architectural designers produce drawings and models, be it electronically or mechanically, to describe a spatial intent that occasionally is translated by others into a building process.

Many designers, and most culturally marginal groups, have up to now not had the opportunity to implement their spatial ideas and have certainly not been able to implement those that have sprung from critical positions.

But architectural design does not have to be consummated by an act of building in order to make a cultural difference. Throughout history the formulation of new spatial possibilities in architecture has primarily been conducted by those working in architectural representation exclusively. This field has always provided a marginal space where experiments could be conducted as cultural changes were under way. Many of these experiments were later accepted as possible realities, as repeated consumption of their resulting images combined with new developments in technology made society more receptive. Moreover many of these experiments changed the existing spatial possibilities and their metaphorical applications profoundly, as demonstrated in the Crystal Chain drawings and the work of El Lissitzky, Etienne-Louis Boullée and Giambattista Piranesi, to name a few "wicked architects" from the past.[1] "To analyze a language thoroughly, it must be isolated, not only from its historical foundations but also from its signifieds. It is not by chance that Piranesi's criticism deeply touches the symbolic pretexts of architectural forms."[2] As built architecture is usually defined by the patrons supporting (and financing) the architectural representation at hand, one can only question the political neutrality of a demand to build a spatial representation at all costs. Even members of academia still seem to be overwhelmed with discomfort when architecture is presented to them without a direct possibility of applying it to the so-called "real" world, a demand they would certainly reject in connection with the majority of their own work, so that they might continue to work critically themselves.

In a critical practice it still seems more appropriate to take things apart through writing than to change conditions through spatial arrangement. I would therefore venture to say that spatial intent need not be validated by building—it can stand instead as a kind of text to be read.

There are many forms of architectural practice.

In the field of representation, architectural practice occupies a gray zone: a space between critical practice (art/writing) and applied practice as conducted within the prevailing political and economic framework. Here Hélène Cixous's demand to write oneself into a world apart from the one that certain white Western males have constructed for us applies.[3] Here one can start one's own critical *architectural* practice: a writing, drawing, model-building practice where a critical discourse can evolve, where the boundaries of the discipline are tested. It is in this realm that we can try "markings, scratchings, scribbling and jotting down."[4]

To the predictable argument that this represents an escape from reality, one can only respond with a counter-model of a possible design practice that though "experimental" is nonetheless versed in the mundane aspects of design and construction, vital to enabling critical action on this very process. To the argument that concentration solely on architectural representation is easier than building, or rather less intellectually demanding, one can only respond that with an acceptance of the status quo, one limits one's possibilities to a framework of a different character but certainly not of a lesser complexity. In fact, the struggle to imagine a spatial possibility appropriate to the chosen framework and the act of representing this possibility in different media remains principally the same, whether built or not.

In the realm of representation we can now stand back and allow for difference. We can produce cracks, fissures, layers, margins, uncertainties. We can rethink spatial hierarchies, and we can experiment with the possibility of a perhaps *other* space. Here one can describe the possible. Here the "what if" is transformed into a critical "if only." The experiment is a tool with which to breach cultural territories up to now neither accessible nor acceptable.

In my own work I often represent the space of fiction, a concept not so very distant from that of cyberspace. Both are governed by representational codes, as Marcos Novac points out in "Liquid Architecture in Cyberspace": "Form is now governed by representation, data is a binary stream, and information is pattern perceived in the data after the data has been seen through the expectations of a representation scheme or code."[5] I do not have any illusions that by producing spatial utopias one will directly influence political and social realities. One can however change expectations of representation schemes, the code of cyberspace, architecture, or any other kind of information. To achieve this, one must represent the possibility of fundamental change in the process of creating space, which might in turn serve as a springboard for other spatial metaphors and perhaps eventually realities.

The protection offered by the academic institution enables the production of architectural representations not defined by their immediate usefulness but by their ability to challenge.

In this practice representation is architecture, contains architecture, and has an architecture of its own.

Within the design process a number of issues arise that beg critical reconsideration. One might, for example, decide to operate within *design*, as certain feminist writers did within the genre of science fiction in the seventies: experimenting within an existing framework, transforming it to produce new work, rather than inventing from scratch. It has proven futile to try to "clear the table" and leave all traces behind, as Walter Benjamin suggested.[6] The tabula rasa approach of many modernist architects can now be read as cleaned-up versions of classicism with sanitary overtones. Inheriting traces must be regarded as something of an inevitable, even desirable, fact.

The question is how to inherit traces rather than to deny that they exist.

In the design process one has actively to search for temporary states of fixity in the shifting territory of representation in order to find form. However, as soon as one defines a spatial representation, the apparent fixity often proves unfixed upon repeated inspection. In response to this slippery state my studio eventually started to experiment with an indiscriminate collection of traces and precedents, which we then transformed through copying, editing, and reinsertion. "Collection" here is understood as a form of practicing memory, not as an attempt to know what happened but as an appropriation of a possible memory culturally denied us.

This process became layered and certainly complex, the recording and analyzing of the different moves and decisions taken along the way a major task.

The following four exercises attempt to both demystify and demonstrate the spatial implications of such a process. Each develops different methodologies of space-making that spring from a profound crisis of belief in inherited compositional traditions.

Authorship, precedence, site, and architecture as shared cultural texts are some of the major aspects of the design process that the studio is reinvestigating.

West Coast Gateway Competition I.
Top, model; *bottom,* plan

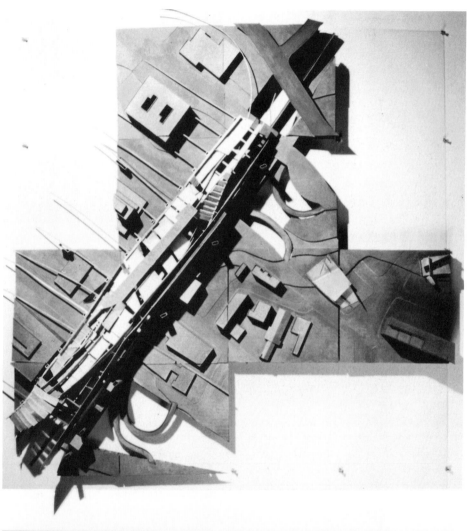

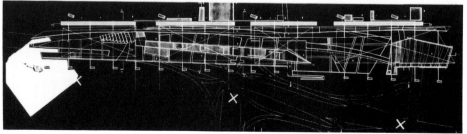

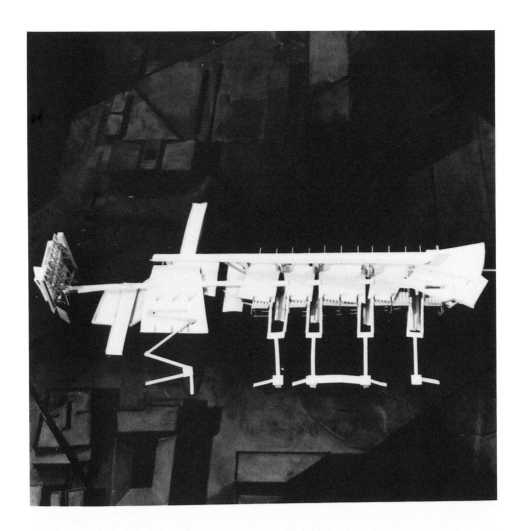

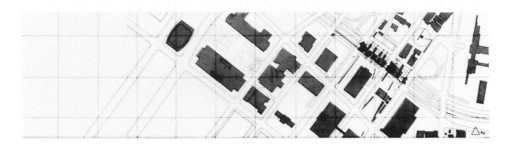

Reading the Site: The Literacy of the Primitive Rebel

The International Los Angeles Gateway Competition, with Shayne O'Neil   Los Angeles has been criticized as having "no there there." This shantytown in the desert is considered a shallow utopia lacking history and people of substance—a description much repeated by mainly European critics that reveals the visitor's blindness and lack of contemporary cultural engagement when baffled by the "L.A. experience." Utopia—nowhere to be found—might be a rather misleading concept here; everywhere to be found—ubitopia—is the reading I would apply. A place where the "there" is a fluidity of so many "theres" that some people seem unable to find a ground.

In this exercise the ordinary physical reality of Los Angeles provides a basis for compositional studies and abstractions. Instead of the idealized orders and images of high architecture, we use the messy, hidden layering of contradictory orders found in the site and the unpredictable reality of permanent change and fluidity. Our inability to adopt commonly accepted precedence created a methodology of space-finding that distills the archaeology of the immediate site and the surrounding downtown Los Angeles.

The Los Angeles Gateway competition brief asked for proposals to reconquer public space above an eight-lane freeway that cut a deep scar into the downtown fabric. This new structure was to be a monument for all immigrants living in the city. In the absence of a functional program, we chose to appropriate it as a gathering space for the public at large and for social services for new immigrants arriving in Los Angeles, none of whom have a collective image with which to identify.

A rereading of the sedimentation on the site revealed various layers directly aligned with different historical conditions. We drew maps of paths, irrigation channels, field boundaries, and building volumes and then collapsed them into a single spatial reading in which all layers are present simultaneously. This collapsed map dictated a new map delineating crevices, volumes, and fields as abstract patterns that could change meaning once, to reiterate Novac, "seen through the expectations of a representation scheme or code."

The different layers of this formal, abstracted landscape are to be viewed from both above and beneath; the extracted forms are placed above the highway in a scaffolding. The most elevated layer, representing recent maps of Los

Angeles's hard asphalt surfaces, was rotated to the vertical, like a drawbridge. This transformation from horizontal to vertical generated a layered wall, a series of surfaces that protect sensitive areas from the highway.

The project presents a conscious veneer architecture. The language of veneer has been used in architectural production since antiquity and has recently reappeared in the work of certain postmodern architects to glue humanist imagery onto structures solely derived from economic forces. However, the concept of veneer—an utter independence between skin and structure—suggests an architecture that goes beyond attempts to pin humanist imagery onto commercial products and promotes a new understanding of ornament. Adolf Loos's curious association of ornament with the primitive and with women is here taken at face value, one of the authors of this project being a woman and the users (immigrants) being permanently devalued and marginalized because of their "primitive culture."[7]

Through the use of veneer architecture, we covered the scar of the freeway with layered platforms, a primitive Potemkin, city allowing spaces in which human activities could reconquer a public domain otherwise surrendered to the automobile.

Phase II: Constructive Possibilities In a second phase of the project, during which many technological and financial constraints were imposed, our interest shifted to constructive possibilities that might define new relationships among the different layers of structure, surface, and volume. Each layer was assigned a specific role and position within the section. The upper layer is for large gatherings. The middle layer is a plant tray where the high traffic on the upper layer is sufficiently unobtrusive for plants to grow. The lowest layer consists of smaller trays that collect water from the thin waterfalls and watersheets flowing through the entire project, acting as an acoustic screen of white noise and an air cleansing system. The volumes penetrating these layers carry folding structures for electrical, water, and information supply.

The Collapse of Hierarchical Thinking: Who is the Author?

An Earthscratcher for Century City As with many other forms of cultural production, architectural production is based on the myth of the individual author, blessed with genius, seduced by the (female) muse. The design process here however reveals quite different possibilities of authorship where a mutual exchange of architectural representations permits the design to be transformed and reformulated by many, rather than one. I do formulate methodologies and experimental frameworks as guidelines for further experimentation; however, the resulting design process depends on the different contributors' choices regarding both metaphorical transformations, translation techniques, and codes of representation.

Implicit in this process is a rereading of the hierarchy of creator and executor, and of structure and ornament. The distinction between building (cultural artifact, male, sovereign, and dominating) and landscape (natural, female, submissive, and passive) has blurred. The hierarchy of structure versus surface has become irrelevant, as the different elements now stand parallel in a nonhierarchical field of fragments.

Several texts emerged at the end of the eighties that reexamine Gottfried Semper's writing on ornament and structure. Many of these theoretical writings were helpful in formulating new methodologies but left open the question of interpreting the many nontextual surfaces experienced daily.

In 1990 I chose Century City, a modernist commercial office development in Los Angeles, as a site for such speculation. Before 1958 this was the site where Twentieth Century Fox Studios constructed and stored an array of simulated environments, including entire cities and lakes made to order. When Twentieth Century Fox Studios faced near bankruptcy in the 1950s, after the box office disaster *Cleopatra*, Welton Becket was hired to create a concept that would transform the back lot of the dream factory into a futuristic city and therefore rescue the film industry via real estate transactions. Today, Century City stands as the ideal product of modernist planning and formal ideology, with its emphasis on effectiveness, cleanliness, open space, verticality, car-oriented infrastructure, and independence from the rest of the city.[8]

Century City proved an interesting text: a sleek, mirrored, antiseptic, and anonymous structure that hides the haphazard, rather tawdry, artificial, and vulgar nature of its previous existence as a film set. The members of my studio made use of a collection of site readings:

Century City's Past Maps of various dates were collected and overlaid. These contained traces and markings of forgotten landscapes: dislocated film towns, movable lakes, film production sheds, oil fields, bungalow structures, and orange groves once again rose to the surface. From these residues we elaborated a new topography of traces that incorporates the previously hidden, which had been bulldozed over by the developers.

Century City's Present

Two recording methods were employed:

1. The shadows of the site—transformed traces of the object of study—were recorded. The shadows manifest a hidden order, an axonometric collapse of the vertical object onto a horizontal projection screen.
2. The sleek skins of the skyscrapers dominating the site were filmed and enlarged to expose the folding and layering in the construction of their apparently smooth and uniform surfaces.

Throughout this process the resulting material daily recirculated among the different authors for reinterpretation. We then tried to divide the fragments produced into two distinct architectural categories: spatial boundaries and infrastructural and structural elements.

Spatial Boundaries: Veneers, Surfaces, and Edges The role of veneer in this project is intimately tied to the site's history: as a ground for filmmaking, conceptually the surface's sole purpose was to provide something that the characters could "fall off of." [9]

But our use of veneer also refers to Semper's rather peculiar and compelling view of the roots of architecture in "Das Prinzip der Bekleidung in der Baukunst" ("The Principles of Clothing in the Art of Building"). Semper discusses the beginnings of shelter and ornament in primitive and more sophisticated societies and insists that the first structures were made of woven branches, which were further developed by woven textile elements, which supplied both shelter and ornament:

[I]t is certain that the beginning of architecture [*Bauen*] coincides with the beginning of textile art [*Textrin*]. . . . The scaffolding, which serves to hold, fix and carry these spatial

Century City project. 1989. *Top,* working drawing (skins and boundaries); *bottom,* photo skin of Century City, city
map.

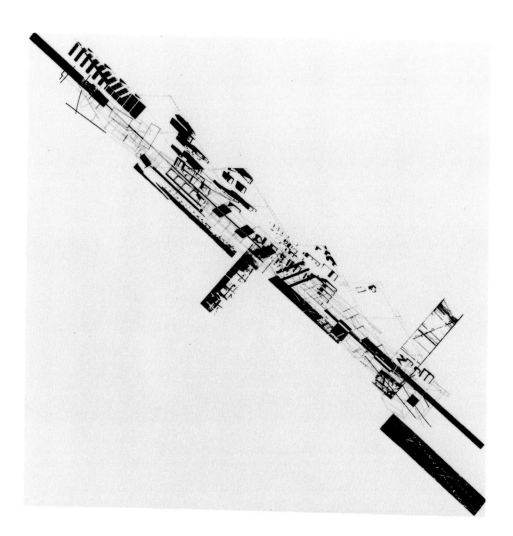

Century City. *Top,* working drawing
(structures and infrastructures); *bottom,* shadow map

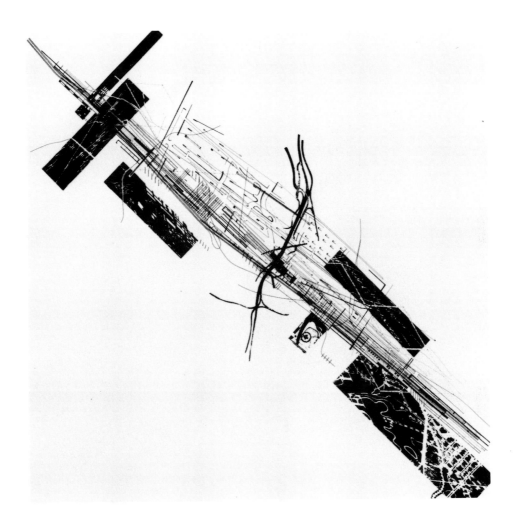

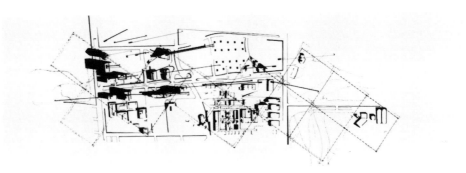

Century City. *Top*, model; *bottom*, working model (skins and boundaries)

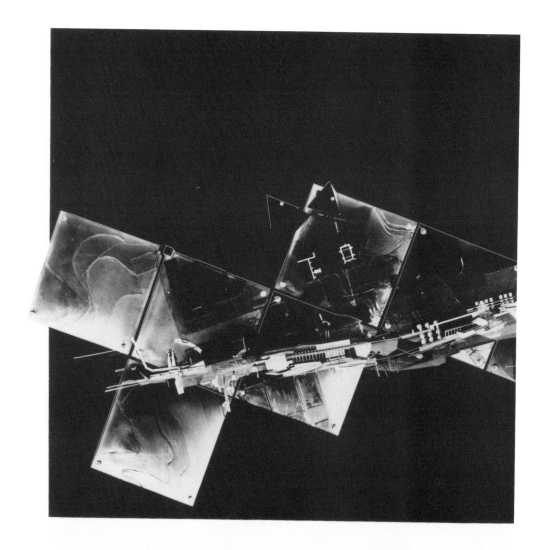

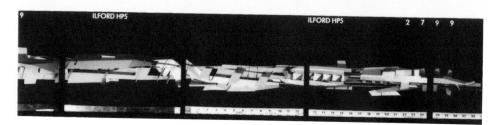

Century City. *Top,* model; *bottom,* plan.

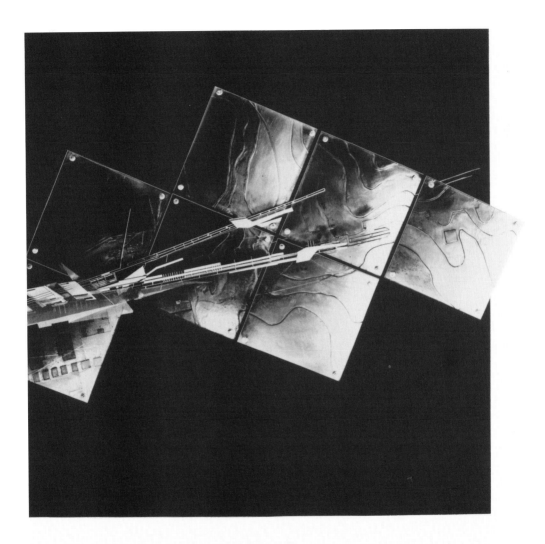

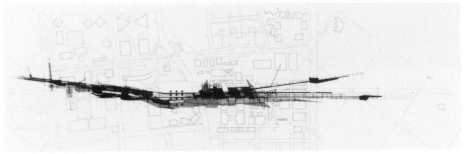

boundaries [the veneer], is a mere necessity that in a direct sense has nothing to do with space and spatial boundaries. It is alien to the fundamental architectonic idea and is at first not an element that defines space.

Semper further points out that in the German language many words describing building elements derive from textile origins. For example, *Decke* means "blanket" as well as "ceiling"; *Wand*, meaning "wall," derives from *Gewandt* meaning "clothing."[10]

This provocative text instigated a rereading, through the design process, of the role of skin and structure and the subtleties of their hierarchical relationship. As the hierarchy predictably collapsed, further experimentation to explore the implications for architectural production became necessary. However, rather than reenact the theoretical text, our response was selective critical appropriation—we simultaneously accepted and rejected Semper's text, interweaving the two responses.

Infrastructures and Structures Construction (Semper's scaffolding) then operates independently in my reading. It is created within the second set of working drawings, where we attempted to read an independent order of structure and infrastructure onto the site. Structure functions only as the scaffolding that holds the skins and spatial boundaries in place. However, in this project, the notion of pure structure is also called into question: the structure here developed an existence of its own, beyond the exclusive task of "holding up." "Structure" and "infrastructure" are used here as independent but generic and formal elements with their own representational roles.

As in film sets and certain recent architectural sections, the importance of the space in between—the space of fasteners, insulation, air buffer zones, and secondary structures—is revealed, space normally marginalized as not "space" but "technical necessity." Within our attempt to question preestablished hierarchies, we chose to treat these in-between spaces in the same way that we had treated the collected surfaces: sections of surrounding and generic skyscrapers were collected and distilled for their structural rhythms, revealing zones defined by technical necessity. The transformation from vertical to horizontal undermined the singular purpose of the structure as simply "holding up" and allowed the repetitive elements to "hold up" in other ways: socially and aesthetically, as well as structurally.

The new model lays itself over Century City's structure as an architectural parasite, living off the "cleanliness" and "open space" of the office development: an earthscratcher that connects the two parks straddling Century City through a set of antiprograms and artificial landscapes in the form of numerous lines, surfaces, and volumes that connect, carry, and shelter human activities. This model is intended as yet another text, available for reinterpretation. It can be read as indicating further spatial development for Century City. It can also be reread by the design team in order further to investigate spaces at a larger scale within an ongoing process of reading and resistive rereading.

The Practice of Laughter: Being Dead-seriously Silly

Rebuilding Beirut: Wrapping up a War

If she's a her-she, it's in order to smash everything, to shatter the framework of institutions, to blow up the law, to break up the "truth" with laughter.
—Hélène Cixous[11]

This project can be seen as an eruption in "hysterical laughter at the absurdity of reason itself."[12] Here we adopted the practice of irony to develop a critical architectural strategy of repair for the city of Beirut.

A collection of maps ranging from antiquity to the fairly recent ruins of French planning allowed us to record a series of layers produced sequentially by catastrophe and repair. Historically in Beirut, catastrophe brought about by human violence or natural disaster has formed a suppressed underlayer in the production of a new architecture. The new structures have chosen to ignore the fact of tragic repetition, each time producing an image of undisturbed unity.

The latest war in Beirut created a "Green Line," an impassable corridor between the Place d'Etoile and the Place des Canons in the center of the city, where the conflict had started. For many years this Green Line in the souks demarcated two halves of the city, divided culturally and politically. This line is now visible by the void that it has created. The development of the surrounding souk area is further hindered by decentralized ownership, which the city's planning elite wants to overcome by massive expropriation.

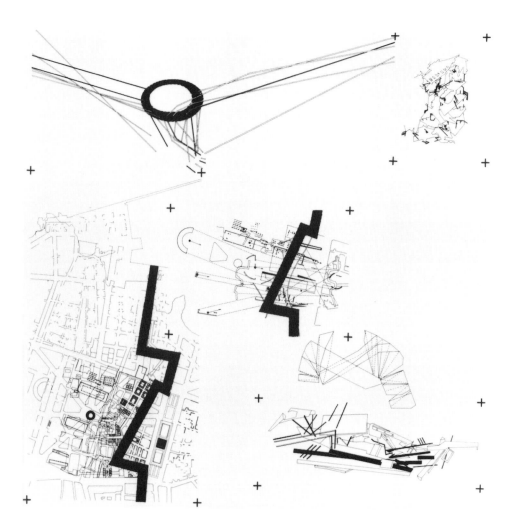

Rebuilding Beirut. Model.

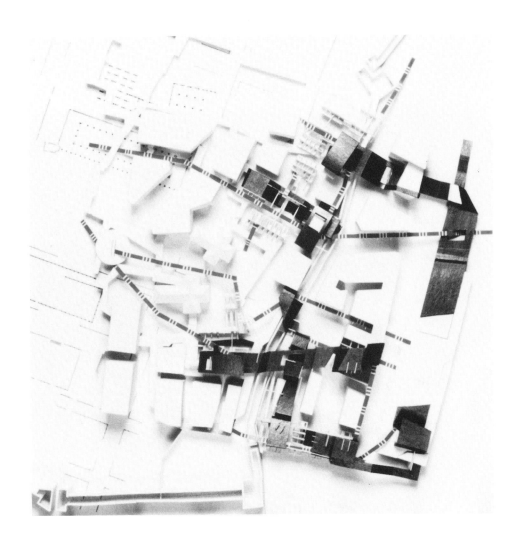

A different approach to "development," however, might choose to reveal the layers of catastrophe, leaving the old operations intact while proposing new structures. This strategy requires new modes of planning: first, an understanding of the existing fabric in section, depicting the layers of previous and proposed operations simultaneously; and second (inherent in this), the courage to leave the scarred areas as found and aid their "development" by strategically adding new layers without insisting on a clean slate.

As a generative device we chose two deliberate misreadings of supposedly unrelated but actually very related operations: the strategies of conventional warfare and conventional medicine. The latter, as embodied in the institutions of healing and disease prevention, came about in response to military developments. The first hospitals were military. Women had always been kept outside the realm of war until the military realized that they were needed to nurture and heal the wounded: the nursing profession was instituted as a direct response to war. The systems of representation used by the nurse and the soldier share a certain language and exploit comparable concepts.

Since the center of Beirut was damaged by constant war, it was more than predictable that the political leadership would call upon the nurse-architect quickly to repair the scarred city. In military terms, a "good repair" would leave the soldier fit for repeated use in combat. The role of the nurse-architect had to be critically reformulated: it was clearly not possible to rescue meaning from the absurdity of war.

We used existing military maps of attack and counterattack to overlay the area with fields of tension and relief for healing purposes. We then used photographs of nurses operating on the city's war victims, where skin was relocated by grafting onto burns and wounds were cleaned and sewn shut, to formulate an aggressive architectural tactic where "strategy" and "operation" are deliberately misread in order to insert new structures into the destroyed areas.

This militaristic medical tactic involved developing an architectural veneer above and around the destroyed souk area, encouraging new growth in the spaces in-between. We proposed a mixture of housing and institutions that could be initiated by the neighborhood's collectively selling air rights above the existing souk area, which would then finance renovation of the area without losing its partitioned and decentralized character. Thin threads of pedestrian bridges create a new three-dimensional urban network, which together with the veneer bandages reconnects the gap left by the Green Line. The new, whimsical suturelike structures originate around the Place d'Etoile and hover above and between the old ruins, while new bandage veneer territories, originating at the Place des Canons, are created by folding and unfolding the earth's surface, revealing previously buried layers underneath and hovering above the souk, adding new layers on top of the scars.

Through this apparently aggressive insertion of new material, a careful repair and transformation of the existing souk area is possible. The structures are developed in such a way that a total recovery to an undisturbed, well-oiled urban structure of visual clarity, ready for combat, is hindered by the simultaneous layering of mutually incompatible structures.

The Art of Copy

Royal Library in Copenhagen, Denmark

The pattern books that are the backbone of architectural production, so that a building can be cooked up from a detail taken from here and a ground plan drawn from there, are just one example of the extent to which aesthetic production has always been at one level the art of making copies from other art.

—Rosalind E. Krauss[13]

Most of the spaces that we experience are random and circumstantial, some of them consciously formulated, most products of chance. We are daily confronted with numerous levels and layers of visual text and physical experience, few of which are produced through any conscious architectural act. The reading of such text manifests itself through making representations of representations—of copying found material. This phenomenon is here employed to shed light on new possibilities for a critical understanding of contemporary space and the use of copying. This study is not intended to define some new style but further to examine a methodology for the creation of form in a time when historical precedent can no longer be used uncritically.

Today Rosalind Krauss's "pattern books" are not the catalogues of the last century to which she refers but the magazines and journals that supply us weekly with new "patterns" ready for common consumption. In academia, a found text is used in quotation marks to serve an argument. The text is then transformed and commented upon to help convey the thesis in question. The

The Royal Library in Copenhagen 1993.
Working plan, reading room perspective, and section.

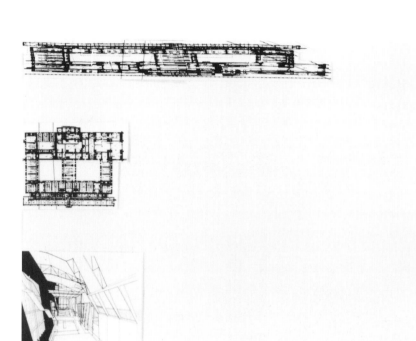

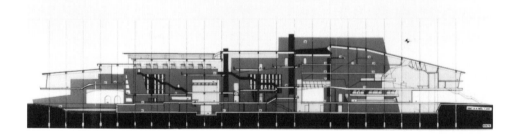

The Royal Library in Copenhagen. Elevation, entrance hall perspective, and plan.

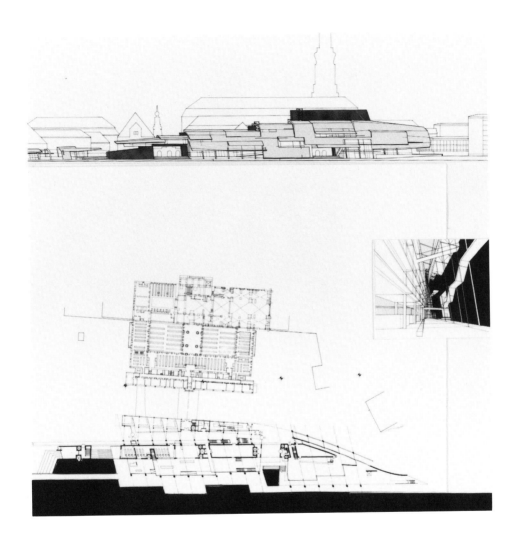

architect, on the other hand, plays the role of fiction writer, concealing and transforming appropriated texts to strengthen the myth of single authorship and of the work as an authentic, original act. This myth provides the author with personal power, which can then be strategically used to promote his right to suppress other views as irrelevant.

In the competition entry for the Royal Library of Copenhagen however, this process became a very conscious and open attempt to establish a methodology based on the art of copy. The brief asked for a "doubling" of the space of the existing library and for proposals to connect it to the inner city and to reorganize a mile-long stretch of the adjacent waterfront.

The Royal Library's role as a conveyor and repository of knowledge and information has been under permanent transition throughout its history. Its mission has changed from a primary protector and administrator of books and objects to an institution that arranges and stores information in multiple ways for mass consumption. Since desktop publishing is now a reality, the diversity and mass of pictorial and textural information has become enormous. Information is produced and distributed more democratically as access to the media becomes easier.

Today information can be stored in electronic units using minimal space. In the future, printed matter will lose its dominance and its spatial requirements. Eventually almost all information will be available without leaving the home. The Royal Library will therefore take on an entirely new role, namely to collect and protect information in order to make sure that it remains accessible to all and to provide a public space for disclosure independent of the institution of the university.

We are now able to read, see, or hear many more and diverse voices previously excluded from the information stream. This has greatly influenced both our architectural production and the questions posed in designing for a new information democracy: How can we best represent multiplicity and diversity in the collection and arrangement of information, culturally and architecturally, without regressing to a neutral architectural frame, devoid of expression? How can we create an architectural representation that speaks inclusively to all members of society?

In a new age of information, we can perhaps hope that some of the prevalent ideologies of precedence and authorship will be dismantled as wider access to certain forms of information slowly undermines the myths that support such beliefs. Our methodology here evolved around that hope.

When the existing library was first planned by architect Hans J. Holm in 1880, it was copied from a foreign ideal, the Royal Library in Munich, which in turn had been copied from a Florentine Renaissance palace. Holm's copy of the found library generated an "ideal" plan, heavily influenced by the Beaux-Arts tradition. Meanwhile the site had been chosen; as a result the architect had to fit his ideal library to a somewhat less than ideal found site containing a rather prominent medieval building. This building, the Galley House, had to be integrated into the new library, which quickly destroyed the autonomy of the Beaux-Arts plan.

However, this found "context" and "history," though regarded as a disturbance, inspired Holm to experiment with translating the borrowed spatial information (the copied library) culturally, so as to represent the Danish identity. The resulting transformation of a clean classical building into an eclectic structure via the enforced integration of existing fabric inspired numerous medieval, neo-Renaissance, and eighteenth-century industrial motifs.

This perhaps insignificant history of the beginning of the Royal Library in Copenhagen shows a break from an established methodology of form making defined by precedence. The tension between the classical tradition and historical accuracy on the one hand and innovation and a search for national identity on the other surfaced even in countries like Denmark, hardly at the forefront of cultural production. Holm, a "Royal Architect" was either unable or unwilling to take up this intellectual challenge for critical reconsideration. Instead he imported a potpourri of motifs from "higher" cultures: a collection of unclassified references compose his "national library."

The building, opened in 1906, was considered a half-executed bilateral cross plan, later to be mirrored in the library garden. The program for the new Royal Library was to double the size of the existing structure. We read this doubling as a mirroring and employed the computer's "neutral" processing techniques to explore an architecture beyond the unconscious collection of precedence. The collection here is highly conscious: the digitized plan of the existing library was stretched to the meet the site's proportions. The original intention of eventually adding a mirror image of the library plan toward the garden to achieve the perfect Beaux-Arts symmetry was appropriated and diverted; the new library mirrors the water instead, foreclosing the possibility of an artificial representation of unity between the two buildings.

We then formulated new rules of translation to meet urban and local conditions: views of and from the city, access from surrounding facilities, security, protection, programmatic requirements, and our determination to create a public forum. These rules were then used to copy, rotate, and cut parts of the new "ideal" plan. The resulting plan generated material for programmatic and spatial interpretation that was then further translated to plan and section, creating a building that exhibits very distinct zones and allows flexibility of function.

The new, stretched library plan consists of strips layered parallel to the water. The program assigned to each strip reflects in mirrored fashion what actually happens in the existing library, the mirroring here being programmatic rather than formal. Zone one, nearest the waterfront, contains the reading rooms. Their shifting rhythms result from the varying proportions of their corresponding formal "relatives" in the existing library. The reading rooms open toward the water and function as a public forum for the arrangement and distribution of information. All reading rooms are located on floating balconies within a large volume. Direct visual contact is maintained between them, much like the balconies in a theater, only the spectacle here is the city itself.

The wall through which one must pass in order to circulate keeps this zone free of traffic and noise. This second zone or information wall is a storage area derived from translating the voids of the library's existing courtyards into a solid wall. The wall is also the organizing element through which the user orients him- or herself and learns how to obtain information and to operate the computer terminals. All information in the form of CDs, electronic storage, books, and objects is stored here in a series of houses within houses within a massive structure; each segment, or house, can be individually closed and locked against light, fire, theft, and climatic dangers. In other words, the wall physically and intellectually "holds everything down," as its dominant presence in the elevation facing the city implies.

The third zone contains all entrance and circulation activities and derives from rotating the fourth zone to accommodate the street, which passes beneath the two buildings. Zone three is defined as a void: one enters the library by slipping sideways into this large, tall space; from here one can reach all ramps, stairs, and elevators to the exhibition halls, the library, the cafeteria, the large concert hall, and the independent institutes.

The fourth and last zone contains administration and reflects the opposite administration wing with its small and repetitive partitions, the mirroring here is both programmatic and formal. All zones in the new and existing libraries are stitched together by two volumes that cut partial voids into both buildings and carry swarms of ramps connecting mutually staggered levels.

The surrounding roofscape from the water's edge was copied and manipulated to produce the elevation's folded surfaces. This copper screen acts as foreground to the parliament building and the existing library's roof. The folded surface can also be read into the roof of the Toejhus Museum adjacent to the library extension: the new library copies the found formal language through abstraction, renegotiating the age-old dichotomy of new and old.

Project Credits

West Coast Gateway, Phase I
Finalist, International Open Urban Design Competition, 1988
Design: Dagmar Richter and Shayne O'Neil
Assistant: Thomas Robertson

West Coast Gateway, Phase II
Third Prize, Invitational Urban Design Competition, 1988
Design: Dagmar Richter and Shayne O'Neil
Assistants: Thomas Robertson, David Adler, Roger Fairey, Eric Lum, Anthony Poon
Engineers: Ove Arup and Partners; Project Engineer: Jane Wernick
Contact Architects in Los Angeles: Ansehn and Allen;
Project Architect: Sarah Dennison

An Earthscratcher for Century City
Independent Research Project, 1990–91
Design: Dagmar Richter
Assistants: Joshua Levine, Theodore Zoumboulakis, Anne Bolneset, Mark Donnahue, Rick Mascia, Cordell Steinmetz, Robert Thibodeau

Rebuilding Beirut
Project for the "Demarcating Lines—Urban Projects for Beirut" exhibition. Exhibited at MIT, 1990 and American University for Beirut, 1991.
Design: Dagmar Richter
Assistants: Theodore Zoumboulakis, Eileen Yankowsky, Anne Bolneset

The Royal Library, Copenhagen
Second Prize, International Urban Design and Building Competition, 1993
Design: Dagmar Richter
Assistants: Nick Capelli, Mercedes de la Garza, Liza Hansen, Carl Hampson, Marc Kim, Scott Oliver, Keith Sidley

Notes

1. I refer here to Manfredo Tafuri's famous essay "'The Wicked Architect': G. B. Piranesi, Heteropia, and the Voyage," in *The Sphere and the Labyrinth*, trans. Pellegrino d'Acierno and Robert Connolly (Cambridge: MIT Press, 1987).

2. Ibid., 39.

3. "Woman must write herself. . . . Woman must put herself into the text—as into the world and into history—by her own movement." Hélène Cixous, "The Laugh of the Medusa," in *New French Feminisms*, ed. Elaine Marks and Isabelle de Courtivron (New York: Schocken Books, 1981), 255.

4. "Cixous challenged women to write themselves out of the world men have constructed from them by putting into words the unthinkable/unthought. The kind of writing that Cixous identified as woman's own—marking, scratching, scribbling, jotting down." Rosemary Tong, *Feminist Thought* (Boulder, Colo.: Westview Press, 1989), 224.

5. Marcos Novac, "Liquid Architectures in Cyberspace," in *Cyberspace: First Steps*, ed. Michael Benedikt (Cambridge: MIT Press, 1992), 234.

6. "Unter den grossen Schöpfern hat es immer die Unerbittlichen gegeben, die erst einmal reinen Tisch machten. Sie wollten nämlich einen Zeichentisch haben, sie sind Konstrukteure gewesen" ("Among the great creators there were always the inexorable, who wanted to clear the table. They wanted to have a clear drawing table, construction was their field"). Walter Benjamin, *Illuminationen* (Frankfurt: Suhrkamp Verlag, 1966), 314 [my translation].

7. "Das ornament der frau aber entspricht im grunde dem der wilden, es hat erotische bedeutung" ("The ornament belonging to women however compares basically to that of the primitive, it derives its meaning from the erotic"). Adolf Loos, *Trotzdem 1900–1930* (Innsbruck: Brenner Verlag, 1931), 203 [my translation].

Also see Adolf Loos, "Ornament and Crime," in *Programs and Manifestoes on 20th-century Architecture*, ed. Ulrich Conrads, trans. Michael Bullock, Cambridge: MIT Press, 1971), 19–20:

> But the man of our day who, in response to an inner urge, smears the walls with erotic symbols is a criminal or a degenerate. . . . In the child this is a natural phenomenon: his first artistic expression is to scribble erotic symbols on the walls. But what is natural to the Papuan and the child is a symptom of degeneracy in the modern adult. . . . *The evolution of culture is synonymous with the removal of ornament.*

8. Thirty years later, after a "successful" planning effort, we confront a "prestige address for business, shopping, luxury living, theater-going, dining and guest accommodation." Century City is described by the local Chamber of Commerce as a landmark for

modern urban development: "One of Century City's most striking features is its architecture. . . . There is a compelling cleanliness about Century City."

9.   "I think we should put some mountains here. / Otherwise what are the characters going to fall off of?" Laurie Anderson, "Big Science," *Big Science,* (Warner Bros., 1982) [lyrics].

10.   See Gottfried Semper, "Das Prinzip der Bekleidung in der Baukunst," in *Der Stil in den Technischen und Tektonischen Künsten, Oder Praktische Ästhetik,* vol. 1 (Frankfurt: Verlag für Kunst und Wissenschaft, 1860), 225–30 [my translation].

11.   Cixous, "The Laugh of the Medusa," 258.

12.   See "Libeskind's Practice of Laughter: An Introduction by Stanley Allen," *Assemblage* 12 (August 1990): 24.

13.   Rosalind E. Krauss, *The Originality of the Avant-Garde and Other Modernist Myths* (Cambridge: MIT Press, 1986), 125.

SITE   CONTEXT

PROGRAM   TEXT

STRUCTURE

VOLUME   BODY

BUILDING   ARCHITECTURE

Chapter 6

DIVERSION Nasrine Seraji-Bozorgzad

Theory / Practice

How important are scenarios in the cinema?

Fellini: You know cinema is image . . . words![1]

Is practice a form given to theory? Is practice the inclusion of theory?

Is practice the construction of theory? Is practice the physical definition of theory?

Is practice not theory?

> *Or les choses se définissent toujours par leur fonction et leur potentialité; quand par suite elles ne sont plus en état d'accomplir leur travail, il ne faut pas dire que se sont les même choses, mais seulement qu'elles ont le même nom.*

> *Since things are always defined by their functions and their potential to fulfill them; when they are no longer capable of doing so, we cannot say that they are the same, only that they have the same name.*[2]

This essay will refer to two projects, one built and therefore touchable, though ephemeral, the other unbuilt and therefore virtual.

Two projects radically different in program and context, extremely similar in thought process.

It is suggested to the reader to think of a cross section, two layers, two plates, in the same way that the architect articulates two floor plans.

Two layers superimposed: the layers are not the same but have common points of reference, a structure that allows the existence of autonomous parts. Solids define voids, voids define solids; both define space, this undefined architectural term.

SITE

American Center The temporary American Center was to occupy a site that belongs to the city of Paris[3] yet is not part of any master plan.[4]

This site in the context of this essay is a nonzone, belonging to no set of rules, no future urban plans, no surveys, no records, no names, and no categories. It lends itself to everything, everyone, nothing, and no one.

A tabula rasa, a void, an undefined place, an *espace trouvé*.

Two years before the completion of the permanent building designed by Frank Gehry, the American Center launched a competition for a temporary headquarters building. Seven young architects were invited to participate; this resulted in my first built work.

CONTEXT

Foyer The foyer for the young, unemployed homeless of Birmingham, England, was to occupy a glorious site, a context of which any architecture student dreams: a canal, a railway bridge, a street, an existing building, romantic and picturesque, yet real. The site is rich in context, poor in reality (a nonspace). An invisible void. A total condition.[5]

Pocket sites in cities, residues of history, unwanted green (gray) spaces or potential parking lots.

Modern architecture needs to insert itself—where better than these residual spaces?

Perhaps we could call this the poetics of *in-between*, the dialectic game of solid and void.[6]

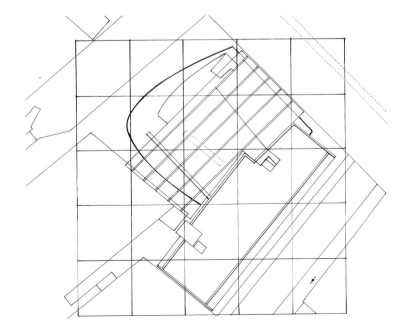

Diversion | **133**

The foyer competition launched by the Architecture Foundation was an experimental project to promote young architects in Great Britain to build and also to encourage an architectural discourse among young practitioners.

PROGRAM

American Center One thousand square meters of symbol, a signature, a bill board, a stunt. The temporary American Center was to play a dual role, that of the actor and the stunt. The stunt is cheaper, short-lived and not recognized, though the stuntman's role is that of the actor.

The building has always been associated with the theater (a theater whose only value is in its excruciating, magical relation to reality and danger), or at least very literally with the stage set. The actors of this theater are the same as that of Frank Gehry's permanent American Center (then under construction), nevertheless their movements are different. As Oskar Schlemmer said to his dancers: the body movement should cut out the interior space of this solid.

The program intrigued me from the start; nothing seemed to be in the correct order, place, or time (cost, construction time, life span, etc.). It could be nothing but an illusion, the Meccano game, which allowed children to believe that construction was only about order and logic and that it could only be red, green, yellow, or blue.[7] The program is a stage set, like almost every other project built in Paris in the past ten years.

Who was it that said, "Theater has given its place to cinema?" Should architecture give its place to literature, philosophy, or perhaps image?

Architecture will always borrow from literature, philosophy, art/image, but it will never be replaced by them, unless we choose to call for the end of architecture.

The temporary American Center was to house all artistic (workshops, studios), educational (classrooms, lecture hall), and administrative (offices) activities of the center on a miniature scale. The center originated from the Left Bank of Paris; the new building on the Right Bank was to portray a new image, an "other" life.

Opposite: There are many models for the foyer in France. The program introduced for Birmingham was to be the first of its kind in Great Britain. The competition related to both theory and practice, discourse and implementation.

TEXT

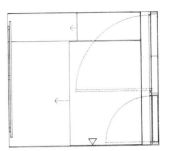

Foyer Two thousand seven hundred square meters of hope, shelter, and home.

The program (developer's brief), contrary to the richness of the site, is a schedule of areas. Despite the optimism of the competition organizers, the competitors find themselves responding to an unrealistic request. On the one hand "space" should be given to the young homeless; on the other, the exigencies of the developers must be satisfied.

What is a competition program? How should architects respond to comments such as, "The program is to be strictly followed unless architecture justifies otherwise." To what extent does *architecture* have the power to ignore the program? Where does the architect draw the line? According to which criteria can architecture justify a diversion? These questions occur and recur in every competition brief. The image, the billboard, and the stunt have the power. Once this magical image has captivated its prisoners, architecture rules.

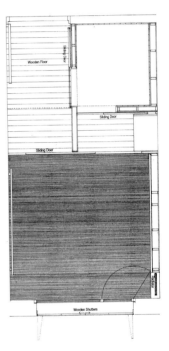

When the program asks for shops, the developer imagines efficient rent return, the competition organizers imagine diversity of facade/image, and the architect thinks of undefined speculative space. Isn't "speculative" a word that contradicts the precision of architecture?

Should architectural ideas be allied with financial interests?

I am scared stiff of people who look at things from the money angle. [8]

If one of architecture's aims is/was to define space and its relationship to the human body, we should (at least by now) have started to acknowledge the virtues of the cubic meter. When was the last time an architect received a program in cubic meters?

In Switzerland perhaps . . . !

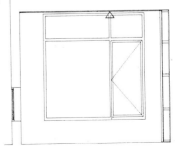

Or perhaps when s(he) needs to design an oil refinery.

Let us give man dignity, not crawl space . . .

Single room (bathroom included): $10m^2$ [9]

STRUCTURE

According to Louis Kahn, structure is the giver of light.

Jean Prouvé says: Never design anything that cannot be made.

In both this essay and in the works presented it is suggested that structure is the connector.

The tension created between spaces, articulated or not, is the role of this connector.

The temporary American Center building relies on and revels in this tension; the nonorthogonal structure/connector attempts to destabilize the order within which it is integrated.

Structure needs to be rational, logical, and preferably perpendicular to the surface of the earth. Why rebel against this tradition? Why allow for misinterpretations? It seems to be the only silent way to establish a dialogue, a dialogue in which architecture asks to be observed and questioned, not just received as a *fait accompli*.

The foyer competition entry deals with structure in a similar yet different manner. Here the visible structure speaks; the apparently heaviest load is supported by the lightest and least conformist structure (a nonorthogonal column carries the glass roof over the central space), a silent political statement.

STRUCTURE

According to Louis Kahn, structure is the giver of light.

Jean Prouvé says: Never design anything that cannot be made.

In both this essay and in the works presented it is suggested that structure is the connector.

The tension created between spaces, articulated or not, is the role of this connector.

The temporary American Center building relies on and revels in this tension; the nonorthogonal structure/connector attempts to destabilize the order within which it is integrated.

Structure needs to be rational, logical, and preferably perpendicular to the surface of the earth. Why rebel against this tradition? Why allow for misinterpretations? It seems to be the only silent way to establish a dialogue, a dialogue in which architecture asks to be observed and questioned, not just received as a fait accompli.

The foyer competition entry deals with structure in a similar yet different manner. Here the visible structure speaks; the apparently heaviest load is supported by the lightest and least conformist structure (a nonorthogonal column carries the glass roof over the central space), a silent political statement.

VOLUME

American Center This projected triangle, this ship, is nothing but the virtual form of the site. If we look closely at the voids between each tree,[10] we can visualize the volumes of the prefabricated modules that house the single offices on the north facade. Their rhythm is anticipated by the context, fifty meters down the road: assembled in two rows are individual houses built in the 1930s (a rare existing condition in central Paris), their individual gardens between them.

The volume was there; the volume will remain (through its absence), once the building is transferred to its future location.

The volume will (would have) change(d), the building will (would have) transform(ed) itself to its future use, its context will (would have) generate(d) its new form. The American Center will (not) be reconstructed, private offices (will not) become cells for the homeless, communal rooms (would have) re-place(d) the meeting rooms, the dining hall (could have taken) takes the place of an exhibition room, the body adapts itself to a new condition.[11]

The dynamics of deconstruction!

The competition winner was announced April 1, 1991. Construction began August 28, and the building was completed on December 18. The building was demolished in March 1994.

BODY

Foyer

The room is the beginning of architecture." [12]

The house is a society of rooms. [13]

The individual is the beginning of humanity. Humanity is a society of individuals.

The foyer is a house for a society.

Autonomy wrapped in a skin, the body of the foyer is made of one hundred individual rooms. Each room has to represent autonomy yet not seclusion.

The room has to offer an "other"; this should be created by the individual. How can the room be planned in order to allow for a volume to announce this "other" life? The volume has to be generous; generosity is related to openness, openness to space. The drawing should express this space.

The rooms rely on each other through a shared space; they open/close themselves to this space, they communicate in a silent manner. [14]

The house is a body of rooms.

Its volume is its presence, though it expresses a desire to disappear.

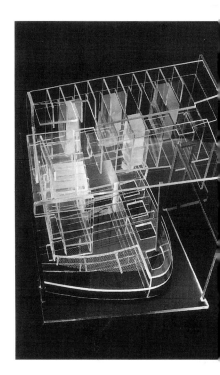

The Birmingham foyer was to provide a role model for other foyers across Great Britain, a program that if successful would have given shelter to many young homeless.

BUILDING

American Center What makes a building a work of architecture? Blanchot's description of the dialectics of a work, "Only if it is torn unity, always in struggle, never pacified, is the work a work," [15] seems the most relevant observation here and could link a building to a work of architecture.

The American Center building desires to be architecture, it demands a dialogue, it allows the inside to be outside, it allows a facade to be two dimensional, it demands to be looked at, it allows itself to be laughed at, it is present.

It stands as a complex trace of many incidents and many confrontations. This is perhaps what has made possible the various critical pieces written on it. It has offered to be seen from many different angles; it is open to all, even the trees.

Architecture has no presence, only a work of architecture has presence. [16]

The American Center building was inaugurated March 21, 1992 (Persian New Year). The internal half-open/half-covered space allowed the first public event to take place under and among the trees.

ARCHITECTURE

Foyer The "constraints and limits"[17] of representation made impossible the presence of the foyer as a work of architecture.

The intentional use of nonhierarchical line (all drawings and spaces are even-handedly represented), the submission of the study model instead of an object-of-desire model, and the confusing three dimensionals played their *stunt role*; this stunt was not appropriately dressed.[18] The aim was to demonstrate an "other" level of understanding of the problem of homelessness.

The practice is young and open to experimentation; we do not intend to represent architectural problematics as a set of multiple choices. The question is to what end do we practice architecture and for how long can the practice resist the nonpractice?

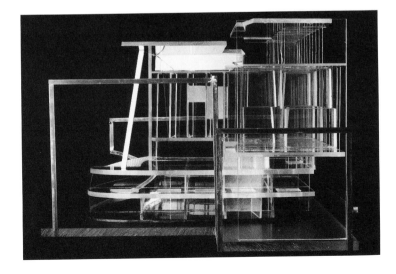

The foyer was to house 120 young home-less, one very large TV room, a dining room, a canal-side bistro, etc. It was to be a large communal house that would prepare its inhabitants for their future.

Epilogue

- In which territory/territories do you operate?

  I am an architect, I build architecture.

- How do you operate?

  In truth and confidence very seldom in solitude.

- How are the personal and the political resolved?

  The personal does not exist, the political is discussed.

- How are theory and practice resolved in your own practice?

  Theory is the spirit therefore untouchable, practice is the flesh and touchable.[19]

Site needs be observed,[20] as Socrates informs Phaedrus in speaking of context,

Socrates

Must I be silent, Phaedrus?—So you will never know what temples, what theaters, I should have conceived in the pure Socrates style! . . . I was going to give you an idea how I should have carried out my work. I should first have set out all the problems, involving a flawless method. Where?—For what?—For whom?—To what end?—Of what size?—And exercising an ever stricter control over my mind, at the highest point I should have realized the operation of transforming a quarry and a forest into an edifice, into splendid equilibriums! . . . And I was drawing up my plan with an eye to the purpose of the humans who pay me; taking into account localities, lights, shadows and winds; choosing the site according to its size, its aspect, its approaches, the adjacent lands and the true nature of the subsoil. . . .

Phaedrus

*. . . **My Temple,** this man from Megara would say, **must move men as they are moved by their beloved.***

Socrates

*That is divine. I once heard, dear Phaedrus, an expression quite similar, and quite the contrary. One of our friends, whom it is useless to name, said of our Alcibiades who was so beautifully made: **Looking at him, one feels one's self becoming an architect!***[21]

Program cannot exist if we do not reconsider truth and the position of humankind; programmers rarely think of humans as the beginning. It is our duty to question the origin and the authority (that it might assume/presume).

Structure is the connector.

Volume need not announce itself, and it will be inherent; its real desire is to be present through its absence.

Building will be architecture when we hear it singing.

Notes

1. Television interview with Federico Fellini. Broadcast Autumn 1992 in France on *France 2*, then *Antenne 2*.

2. Pierre Ansay and René Schoonbrodt, *Penser la ville* (Brussels: AAM Edition, 1989), 138. From this collection of essays on the city by philosophers, this part is an extract from "The Politics of Aristotle" under the heading "The State and the Individual." This quote refers particularly to the context of things and the notion of displacement. I have retained the French because of its grammatical division and clarity; the translation given is mine and remains closer to the French sense relevant here. Aristotle, *The Politics*, trans. T. A. Sinclair (London: Penguin Classics, 1962), 60–61, 1253 a1., contains the authorized translation:

> Furthermore, the state has a natural priority over the household and over any individual among us. For the whole must be prior to the part. Separate hand or foot from the whole body, and they will no longer be hand or foot except in name, as one might speak of a "hand" or "foot" sculptured in stone. *That will be the condition of the spoilt hand, which no longer has the capacity and the function which define it. So, though we may say that they have the same names, we cannot say that they are, in that condition, the same things.*

3. The site is the property of the city, a public square; no private building could theoretically occupy it.

4. Paris is largely divided by a general zoning plan *(Zone d'Amenagement Concertée* [ZAC]); the master plan is designed by the architect(s) of the ZAC.

5. By referring to total condition I am emphasizing the utopian nature of the site and program for the foyer.

6. Discussions with a dear friend and architect, Jacques Sautereau.

7. Meccano was the predecessor of Lego, a (subtle and intelligent) game of construction using flat metal sections with punched holes in order to allow for construction joints with a system of nuts and bolts (my favorite childhood pastime).

8. Louis I. Khan, *Writings, Lectures, Interviews*, introd. and ed. Alessandra Latour (New York: Rizzoli, 1991), 191.

9. From the foyer competition program distributed to all competitors, first line after the introductory pages on what a foyer represents in France and what it should be in the framework of this competition. Programs rarely (almost never) question the qualitative nature of spaces desired; rather, they treat the quantitative aspect.

10. There are three rows of existing trees on site: two rows on the periphery, one row along the center line. The "void volume" between the trees filled by the individual office modules refers to the two rows on the periphery and the space between them.

11. At the time of writing this essay negotiations were taking place between various parties in order to transfer the building to another site and renovate it for use as a temporary shelter for the homeless. Politics and the law of precedents did not allow this.

12. Khan, *Writings, Lectures, Interviews,* 294.

13. Ibid, 294.

14. The foyer program required one TV room for every four bedrooms as a communal space for the occupants to communicate and interact. We decided that the television was not the instrument of communication among the young unemployed homeless. Each bedroom shares a kitchen and communal sitting/gathering area, as an alternative response.

15. Maurice Blanchot, *The Space of Literature,* trans. Ann Smock (Lincoln: University of Nebraska Press, 1982), 229.

16. Khan, *Writings, Lectures, Interviews,* 221, 248.

17. The panel (judges') report on the foyer competition declared our drawings unreadable. The decision to draw all lines with the same pen renders reading extremely difficult; I am talking about the limitations and constraints of representation and hence readability.

18. I refer to the beginning of the essay: the role of the "actor" and the "stunt"; here architectural representation becomes the stunt.

19. These questions were part of the brief for this piece, asked of each author by the editor.

20. From where should my building be viewed? Perhaps from the inside. In fact it *has* to be viewed from the inside; isn't this the only way to perceive space?

21. Paul Valéry, "Four fragments from Eupalinos or the Architect," in *Selected Writings of Paul Valéry,* trans. William McCausland Stewart, (New York: New Directions, 1964), 165, 183.

Chapter 7

LOSING IT IN ARCH$_{IT}$**ECTURE:
OBJECT LAMENT**

Catherine Ingraham

Recently I was working on a piece of writing in which I was trying to untangle the famous aphorism "a picture is worth a thousand words." The more I tried to penetrate this equation, the more peculiar it became. We know, generally, the circumstances under which this phrase is uttered—circumstances where a certain crisis has arisen between two values, the value of the word and the value of the picture (to which we could append everything grasped visually).[1] Although the import of the aphorism is that it takes many, many words to achieve what a picture can achieve all by itself, at once, one thousand words is low when it comes to words. One thousand words represents about three pages of written text, about six minutes of continuously spoken language, about ten minutes of conversation. One thousand pictures (and a million words), or one

one-thousandth of a picture (and one word), would be a more accurate way of stating the force of this aphorism. The issue of value and worth, so slyly persuasive in this equation, is related, then, not to some carefully weighed economy of words and images but to a tacit politics of expenditure that counts words as cheap and insubstantial and therefore proliferative and images as substantial and dear and therefore unique.

I am belaboring this aphorism because I am interested in the equation between words and images, words and things, words and objects. And, also, I have felt blamed by this aphorism for a long time. At the same time I recognize the ugliness and difficulty of words compared to things—how small and petty words are, how snakelike and promiscuous. This ugliness is part of what aesthetically magnetizes me about words. Taking the aphorism at face value is, paradoxically, an oblique way of looking at a far more difficult set of problems having to do not only with the particular kind of architectural practice that might lead us to question the economy between words and things but also with the realm of *invention*. I am bringing this word into this text because it is a key word in Francesca Hughes's proposal to those of us invited to submit something to this book. The proposal was that women had more cause to invent an architectural practice because they hold an ambiguous position with respect to architecture—they are both outside and inside architecture.[2] It might be that women have a kind of historical affinity for invention and ambiguity, an affinity that would have to include the forces of necessity, whatever they might be. But let me return for a moment to the aphorism "a picture is worth a thousand words." The spirit of the aphorism recognizes the mediating function of words and the apparently unmediated meaning of the image. The attempt of words to represent pictures or images or objects, according to this aphorism, not only happens outside the image or object (as a kind of excess of clothing around the image or object) but results in a proliferation of multiplicities (one thousand) that is offensive to the apparent singularity of meaning that is the picture, image, or object. The themes that we might locate here—the mediation of meaning, competition between outside and inside, the ever-present problem of representation, systems of value, the frame and its economy, multiplicity and singularity, the politics of meaning—are part of my architectural practice, and I think they belong to everyone practicing a critical architecture today. The material implications of these themes—that is, what can be built from them—are not as elusive as both theorists and practitioners make them out to be. Materiality is relatively easy; it lays in wait for metaphysics and philosophy at every turn.

Taking an aphorism at face value is tactically adiaphoristic; it breaks into the formal closure of the aphorism. But taking something at face value is also a material moment, in the sense that it deals with the formal and material propositions of something—the dimensions, quantities, literalness of that thing (in this case, language). The sense in which language, say, is revealed to have a surface meaning that casts doubt on its deeper purposes is peculiar since language is nothing but surface to begin with, although we know that the "nothing" in the "nothing but surface" must also be taken into account.[3] In fact, everything is nothing but surface. But there are two especially potent surface structures: the first is language (as the aphorism, even in its less-than-literal spirit, knows), and the second is architecture.

Let me quickly review the grammatology of this situation, quickly not because it is irrelevant but because Derrida is so powerfully present in all that one says about language that this essay could quickly become an apology to Derrida for saying what he says, only in a worse way, and I don't think this is the place for examining that particular pathology. And, also, by now, everyone knows all this. But there is one piece of this pathology that bears mentioning. That one thing leads to another in philosophy or any kind of work, such that everything is formed on already existing forms (either as the sort of extensive cross-referencing in which philosophy engages or the matter of architectural precedent) is a fact that architecture has found both appealing and appalling throughout its own history. I say this because whenever I return to Derrida in the middle of a discussion about architecture, I am reminded of how completely thought and action must already be structured in order to operate. Derrida's insights on structuring and structurality are staggering, and architectural theory was right, I think, to have found a (troubled and temporary) home in Derrida inside the problem of structure.

On our way back to the aphorism, then, through Derrida: it is not enough to say that words are the other of the image, or vice versa. One must further divide words into spoken and written words. Written language is the image of speech.

Has it ever been doubted that writing is the clothing of speech? . . . One already suspects that if writing is "image" and exterior "figuration," this representation is not innocent. The outside bears with the inside a relationship that is, as usual, anything but simple exteriority. The meaning of the outside was always present within the inside, imprisoned outside the outside, and vice versa. Thus a science of language must recover the *natural*— that is, the simple and original—relationships between speech and writing, that is, between an inside and an outside.[4]

The clothing of speech by writing, the clothing of images with words, produces a perplexing shift between what we have always held to be exteriority (images) and what we have always held to be interiority (language, most specifically speech). To extract one more turn from this most salient of passages on writing: Derrida speaks of our attempt to recover the natural relationship between inside and outside, which would have been "inverted by the original sin of writing." The mythology of an original speech that was later sullied by writing, civilization, genealogical anxiety is the mythology and theology of the Garden of Eden itself, which was, above all, a place where inside and outside were fixed. Derrida goes on:

Malebranche explained original sin as inattention, the temptation of ease and idleness, by that *nothing* that was Adam's distraction, alone culpable before the innocence of the divine word: the latter exerted no force, no efficacy, since *nothing* had taken place. Here too, one gave in to ease, which is curiously, but as usual, on the side of technical artifice and not within the bent of the natural movement thus thwarted or deviated.[5]

The nothing that is Adam's distraction presumably falls under the sway of Eve and the serpent's argument. Their argument is already set against the grain of the natural and thus already represents a fissure in the inside/outside structure of the garden. Eve herself is the preoccupied agent of writing (the agent of the Fall). She is doubled by the serpent with its writhing unfixity. Adam's distraction falls on Eve's preoccupation and is directed along the surface of that preoccupation to its fateful end. This nothing/distraction/surface cathexis is, in some autochthonic way, a mythological preparation for the "nothing but surface" that describes the cathexis of subject and object relations in Jacques Lacan (see note 3). Surface is the place of distraction. This technical artifice that is nothing but surface is, in Derrida, writing (*arche-writing*[6]) and also any other mark of culture. Paradoxically, once things are recognized as surfaces, things surface—we get a look at what lies deeply within.

Francesca Hughes has suggested that women are more likely to invent a practice in architecture. The spirit of her suggestion is that women invent a way into architecture by inventing different practices, for example, careers in theory rather than building careers. We cannot ignore for a moment the problem of the object, most specifically the architectural object, implicit in this example. While it would be a kind of theoretical folly to pursue the history of the built object with respect to some generalized gender condition called "woman," a number of mythologies, theories, and histories situate women with respect to objects. Generally these mythologies provide conflicting accounts of women and objects. Some suggest that women are acquisitive of objects and are themselves objects to be acquired; others that women are expert purveyors of words but have an imperfect or weak relationship to objects. Words are cheap, objects are dear—except where the woman herself is an object, in which case objects are cheap too. Women acquire objects, but they produce words. One could mention, as always, Penelope, the shroud, the suitors, Helen and Paris, of course Scheherazade and her endless tale, certain African societies that equate women with semiprecious objects, the relation of women to jewelry and money, property ownership histories, domestic engineering, Melanie Klein and other object theorists, the adjectives that have traditionally described women's speech/objects such as babble/bauble and chatter/chattel, Jacques Lacan, contemporary feminist theories of female identity, and so on. As we would discover in different ways from these investigations, and as we already know from the spin of the aphorism "a picture is worth a thousand words," the opposition between words and things or words and objects is impossibly difficult to uphold and, more specifically, to genderize. The opposition between words and things, which is also the opposition between theory and practice, behaves like many oppositions of this kind: "What is most characteristic of these oppositions [word versus things] is that as soon as you put pressure on them they break down. Each time one element of a pair is driven into a corner, it changes shape and frequently turns into its opposite."[7] The more one attempts to be clear and emphatic about these oppositions, the more certain they are to become entangled in each other. Yet we know that summarized under the heading theory/practice is an entire range of practices that feel confident about differentiating themselves from each other. The more one tries to show the mix-up of words and things, the more calcified the distinction between them becomes. I know most of the stock answers why this is so—answers having to do with the status of the object in Western consciousness and so forth. But here I want to propose another answer having to do with a particular spectrum of gender effects that belong specifically to America.

Wherever we find a specific group of people almost entirely excluded—in this case, women from the profession of architecture—we might suspect that there is some kind of identification crisis underway. Architecture is not, contrary to its reputation, an object profession. Very few architects actually build, in a physical way, the buildings they design. It is a profession of object thinkers who grapple with the living condition of the object as a condition terminally other to itself. The carpenter or electrician—the trade person who actually carries out the instructions specified by the architect—is a different order of being from the architect, and this is testified to by the massive legal, cultural, and material conflict between these two worlds. What the architect has is "knowledge of materials," and this knowledge is in perpetual negotiation with the actual material practices that the architect must marshall to his/her cause. I don't want to explore here all of the multiple dimensions of how architects identify with the construction of the buildings to which they never literally put a hand, except to say that the sense of object loss or object lament is a very long and deep strand in architectural history. I want only to touch on this history obliquely by means of another history, the mythical history of the American West.

Jane Tompkins writes of how, in the film genre of the western, a certain concept of the masculine was aligned with the need to become as total, as dense, and as present as an object. She quotes Peter Schewenger: "To become a man . . . must be finally to attain the solidity and self-containment of an object." [8] And she quotes Octavio Paz, whose definition of "macho" is a "hermetic being, closed up in himself." "The interdiction masculinity places on speech," Tompkins says, "arises from the desire for complete objectivization. And this means being conscious of nothing, not knowing that one has a self . . . nature is what [the hero] aspires to emulate: perfect being-in-itself." [9]

The western film is, of course, a parable of American identity that bears specifically on the settling of the West and the relationship of men and women to that settlement. In this parable, women are the protectors of proper speech, which is the speech of the schoolteacher and the society woman imported from the East. The identification of women with proper speech is synonymous with the proprietorial role women played in the West as those who settled a mobile population into proper houses, schools, towns with libraries, and so forth.[10]

But the house itself, the building and ownership of the house, belongs to the other side of the parable, the man's side. Owning property, which was, of course, part of what the settlement of the West involved, was related in some intimate way to the male identification with land as object. Turning the West into real estate, and subsequently towns and cities, required both the "silent" identity with objects (the image) and the "talkative" identity of social propriety (the word). This has never been, however, a happy or harmonious marriage. Architecture's identification crisis, at least in part, belongs to a version of this parable.

The sense in which architecture stands back from the object guarantees the anxiety associated with the admission of women into its ranks. For mastery over the object—becoming one with the object—is not possible in architecture (in fact, it is possible nowhere), and women have traditionally almost always stood for the failure of that mastery. To invite women in is simultaneously to invite in the idea that the (mistaken) route to masculinity through architecture and the object will be foreclosed. The architecture of the American West—the scene of Tompkins's observations—is a landscape of solid monumental forms (buttes, mesas, etc.) against a horizon. In search of perfect objecthood and the hermeticism of *machismo,* the western hero tries to assimilate himself totally to this landscape. But this architecture—and now we see it is a mistake to call it architecture—is *nothing like* the architecture of the architect. The architecture of architects is hollow inside, not dense, not solid. So if the paragon of American (and to some extent, European) masculinity, the western hero, falls short of becoming one with the densely formed landscape, how much more does a voided architecture fail to deliver its object promises.

Women are on the surface of architecture. They are nothing to architecture. They are active participants in the etiology of distraction. But like Adam's distraction, the "nothing that happens" between women and architecture is, nevertheless, a provocation that results in a fall from the "bent of the natural." Women invert something, by being nothing, not because of some hidden or gender-specific power but because architecture itself is nothing but surface. There is a strange isomorphism between the surface and face practices of women (their adiaphoristic and wordy practices) and the practice of architecture. While I am not speaking of the feeling of nothingness to which most women testify as the shape of their identity, an account of this feeling might curiously accord with the nothing of distraction, of surface, of face value, of language, of technical artifice. Women, like writing, are in an always already fallen position with respect to architecture.

But, of course—we must say it again—it is a dead end to isolate some generalized (object) position for women or men. Jacqueline Rose, in the introduction to Lacan's *Feminine Sexuality*, writes:

Sexuality belongs in this area of instability [arbitrary nature of language] played out in the register of demand and desire, each sex coming to stand, mythically and exclusively, for that which could satisfy and complete the other. It is when the categories "male" and "female" are seen to represent an absolute and complementary division that they fall prey to a mystification in which the difficulty of sexuality instantly disappears. . . . Lacan therefore argued that psychoanalysis should not try to produce "male" and "female" as complementary entities, sure of each other and of their own identity, but should expose the fantasy on which this notion rests.[11]

Instead of speaking of "women" we should speak of the unstable and shifting equations produced by the conjunction architecture + female + male + architecture, etc.; and we would have to specify which part of architecture we meant, and so on. This would be the project that would discover what the ambiguity of outside/inside and invention might mean for women in architecture.

But I am not officially an architect. These words are uttered by many, not simply those who, like myself, swerved into architecture from another field; those who are, essentially, self-taught in architecture. Leon Krier has a version of this same disclaimer that argues that architecture is so corrupt that it is a scandal and an embarrassment to be associated with the field (he's right, but wrong). The fact that I am not a (bona fide) architect suggests many things to the architectural imagination. It is not surprising that some of the work I do in the world of critical theory is concerned with issues of propriety and impropriety, although I feel this is the crudest possible linkage between a professional characterization and a theoretical thematic (but, as we shall see, no one is more crude than the autobiographer—nothing is cruder, psychologically speaking, than autobiography). I have invented a practice and, to some degree, its terms. It would not be quite accurate to say that I invented a practice because I was female and, therefore, outside, since, as Derrida reminded us, to be outside is never a simple exteriority, especially in the case of women whose history in contemporary culture has been as a thing of appearances and faces. The discourse in which I was interested at the time of this invention was, one might say, one that took invention as one of its main themes; invention as a bogus origination, a contrivance. And, further, I was able for a time to benefit by being in the twilight zone between two professions. The full-blown philosophical position that I brought into architecture from literature and literary theory, where it had, in turn, been imported not from philosophy but from a handful of philosophers, found architecture strangely unguarded. It was as if architecture had forgotten all of its theoretical history and all of its intellectual life, so taken by surprise was it by this imported discourse. This surprise did not last long, but it lasted long enough to infuse much of this theoretical work with the tactics of surprise. I am not speaking simply of my personal part in this drama since, at that time, there were a number of people—perhaps six or seven men and women—who were doing the same thing in different ways. Now, of course, we are in a different period, for those of us who were outside eight years ago, and the discourses that were then outside, are now inside. But this too cannot be a simple interiority. There have been significant contortions.

The one question that governed, and continues to govern, my thinking is not, as one might suspect, literary or in any obvious way philosophical. It is the question, enunciated in the middle of theoretical work: "What has this got to do with architecture?" This chilling question, this question that casts a (paternal) chill on the whole enterprise—that solidifies the wandering subject into a narrow set of prosaic concerns about space, line, ornament, inhabitation, design, structure, etc.—is uttered at the moment of peak anxiety about the path of a piece of work. The building up of anxiety around the question "what does this have to do with architecture?" is like the parent responding to the child's outrageous desires, the interruption of the pleasure principle under which the child is operating. The "what has this got to do with . . ." is the moment of discipline, restraint, moral consciousness and, also, inevitably, the moment at which all dangers of cultural construction, socialization, and political conformity assert themselves. The profession of architecture, at the outset, plays the parent to theoretical work, but the ending to the tale is not quite so easy to summarize. What begins as a seemingly inflexible demand to make what is loose and far-fetched meaningful and substantive in architectural terms often ends as a seduction of architecture by its other, an other that the invention of theory both stands for and speaks about. The question "what has this got to do with architecture?" it seems is infinitely infiltratable by the nonarchitectural, indeed is constituted in the terms of the infinitely open existential question "what is . . ." Thus does the animal, the angel, the slime mold, the color white, the garment, the Jeffersonian grid, the labyrinth, the woven cloth, the play, the book, the worm, the bed, the airplane, the mask, music, dance— the whole skein of irrelevant subjects that one finds theorized in architecture throughout its history—thus do these irrelevancies come to constitute the properly architectural at one moment or another. The otherness of architecture to the apparently nonarchitectural is like the otherness of the male to the female—not able to be held in place unless the difficulty of desire is removed by the absolute division of (architectural) identities and (architectural) objects.

The chill isn't quite done away with, even when the seduction is complete, because the chill in the case of my work is not solely cast by the rhetorical question "what does this have to do with architecture?" but also by the latent suspicion that someone, who is not a bona fide architect, is claiming something on behalf of architecture; this is the chill of the absent building, which, as we know, is "indisputedly architectural." All that happens in writing falls shy, in the eyes of architecture, of the building, no matter how much we might mine the implications of the promiscuous word *structure* in all of its places. This new form of anxiety, building up around the building and its absence, is the one that most bedevils the architect who is separated from the other architects by the name *theorist* or *critic*. This is not about simply wandering away from the subject at hand but about being in the wrong medium altogether, like trying to breathe air if you are a water animal, or the difference between having blood and chlorophyll. This is *species and kingdom* anxiety. For those of us who are theorists . . . no, let me speak for myself . . . for myself, who has gotten used to, indeed partially invented and then inhabited, the persona of the architectural theorist, this species anxiety is very interesting, very telling. To recall earlier discussions in this essay, the anxiety surrounding building in architecture is intimately associated with all of the themes that belong to visual/verbal economies and with the mix-up of sexual identity and objects. And, also, with yet another theme: the pleasures of lament, which is a kind of new objecthood (crudely, the pleasures of being limited by "reality"[12]).

As I have already suggested in a different way, the building, rather than being a positive acquisition, is the site of loss, the site of a lament. This lament, in turn, fuels a new critical practice (in the midst of construction, so to speak) that saves itself from the debilitating power of loss by adopting a tone of matter-of-factness, of the self-evident.[13] The other, covert, face of lament, then, is "description"—a particular kind of speech (and geometry) meant to establish without question and verify without gap the presence of the object in space, the building, the body, the thing, whatever. The shop drawing is perhaps the most banal of descriptive documents; the architectural rendering, or perhaps architectural history, the most exalted. The force of the described is the force of something whose self-evidence is so great that the speech used to name it is the speech of recognition—*here is the building; well, yes, so it is; let it be so; here is the stone, here is the brick, here is the window*—and the recapitulation of a certain journey around and through it—*then we walk down a corridor, then we descend some stairs, then we enter a room.* The apparent spareness of this descriptive speech, like the speech of the western, is a spareness about erasure. Descriptive language is trying to erase itself, to disappear into the object, the building. Its desire is to become the building and, like the will-to-silence of the western hero, it is the language of (masculine) aspiration toward objecthood. Of course this never happens. If anything, the reverse happens. The more one tries to have the building, the more wordy things become. That is, the more the language of description fails to deliver the object, the more the language of lament steps in to reclaim the object as an object of loss.

The act of design is precisely like the analytic act of recapitulation—it is a labored spelling out of things next to things next to things toward the proleptic completion of the whole. If, as I have been trying to argue, the building is the site of a gap filled up, provisionally, with the multiple descriptions that create a web of reality, who is responsible for the dynamic of this deception? The architect? The theorist? Both, of course. But also the condition of loss itself that, through the techniques and strategies of the lament, weaves the web that is its own cover-up.

The lament relationship between objects and words brings them into an intricate and ongoing play of desire that both confines and defines each. This is, at least in part, where the architectural theorist resides, where she invents a practice. The particular problem that inaugurated this essay was the problem of trying to figure out the significance of "a picture is worth a thousand words." What now seems true of that aphorism is that it is hiding yet another meaning: *a picture is worth a thousand laments* or, perhaps, *a picture laments a thousand words.*

Notes

1.   But what would we do with the written word? Is it too a picture?

2.   Francesca Hughes suggested that this "architecture" be rendered "Architecture" with a capital *A* to indicate the entire culture of architecture—the profession, the discipline, the building. She wanted to underscore the idea that invention is not utopic in the sense that it points to some more idealized state of female practice with respect to architecture. I agree with her, but I have an aversion to a capitalized architecture. Perhaps, in some unexamined way, lowercase architecture signifies for me the massive plurality of architectural meanings in the field, the discipline, the building, and beyond. This "beyond" is important. Also, *A* cannot be capitalized with impunity insofar as we are warned by Derrida against the "kingdom of the a, the silent tomb, the pyramid."

3.   The formulation "nothing but surface" refers to Lacan's "rejection of any mythical notion of the unconscious as the seat of instincts, a rejection of any sort of depth psychology. The subject—that is, the subject revealed by psychoanalysis—is to be understood simply as an effect of the signifier, a subject of the letter." Jean-Luc Nancy and Philippe Lacoue-Labarthe, *The Title of the Letter, A Reading of Lacan,* trans. François Raffoul and David Pettigrew (Albany: State University of New York Press, 1992), 10. The "nothing" must be taken into account because it is, of course, too glib to say that everything is nothing but surface since the very enunciation of this principle is itself calling on a forgotten substance or a forgotten depth, a refused depth.

4.   Jacques Derrida, *Of Grammatology,* trans. Gayatri Chakravorty Spivak (Baltimore: Johns Hopkins University Press, 1974), 36 [Derrida's emphasis].

5.   Ibid, 35 [Derrida's emphasis].

6.   Arche-writing is writing before the letter (avant la lettre) and therefore includes speech. I want to remark here on how this word *arche* now strikes me as strange. Intermingled with the word *arch* as a noun (curved structure supporting . . .), as a verb (span), as an adjective (chief, preeminent, facetiously serious), and as a prefix (chief, superior, as in arch-deacon, "first," "original"), the word *arche* in, say, architecture (*arch-builder*), has been used regressively. Paolo Soleri (Arcosanti), Archigram, etc. use the sense of the *arche* as a recovery of some primal condition of architecture (as craft, as carefully built object). In architecture, arche-writing would signify a "return to origins" rather than the critique of origins it is meant to be. Most of Derrida's neologisms *technically* (and deliberately) belong to the epoch of the philosophical suffix *-ology* (phenomenology, grammatology, ideology); the epoch of the Logos. But arche-writing belongs in some odd way to the sixties and the "return to nature" nomenclature of that time, which was also the source of some of architecture's "arch-" movements. Not in any literal sense, of course, since the so-called return-to-nature movements in America during the sixties were regressive in all of the ways that Derrida's assaults on logocentrism are meant to reveal.

7.   Jane Tompkins, *West of Everything: The Inner Life of Westerns* (New York: Oxford University Press, 1992), 48.

8.   Ibid., 56.

9.   Ibid., 56.

10.   The prostitute, who preceded the "proper woman," is not usually depicted as antithetical to the female project of settlement. Her house is lavishly and permanently furnished and she "entertains." Men have to get clean of the land before they go to this house, and their manners matter. But, strictly speaking, the prostitute is a woman who wanders and, in this, she resembles the man who wanders. Her wandering, however, never results in property ownership because she neither settles down like the woman nor identifies with the land like the man.

11.   *The Woman in Question*, eds. Parveen Adams and Elizabeth Cowie (Cambridge: MIT Press, 1990), 33.

12.   I am thinking, at the moment, of Robert Venturi and Denise Scott Brown's *Learning from Las Vegas*, where they enumerate in great detail the loss of complexity in the face of the real. This text is filled with the pleasure of lament.

13.   I have personified the lament here because, in my first encounter with it, the lament was a young girl in a Rilke poem (the *Tenth Duino Elegy*). See Catherine Ingraham, "Architecture: The Lament for Power and the Power of Lament," *Harvard Architecture Review* 8, ed. Peter Coombe (New York: Rizzoli International, 1992). In that article, what I find interesting about the lament is that it seems to find a special kinship with architecture. It is helpful that Rilke offers us a female lament since I have been arguing in this essay that women also have a special kinship with architecture.

INVISIBLE LINES

Christine Hawley

If I had spent the last twenty years rooted in a building site, I am sure my attitude would be different.

I essentially live in a world of the imagination and am fascinated by how it might be realized. I am not persuaded by ideas for ideas' sake, though I am intrigued by the creation of analogies to the architectural condition. I am less interested in ideas that seem unlikely to be fulfilled, though I don't object to speculation. My attitude probably arises through working in a world saturated by ideas—often very obscure ideas—and in which the culture of imagined architecture is seen as a rhetorical art form.

I would like to think that my work is *craftsmanlike* rather than academic. Naturally this has many implications, not least that it is based upon experience: difficult if one does not build enough. Experience can to some extent be augmented by enthusiastic observation, looking again and again at objects and situations that are fascinating and each time noting some further facet of their craft—or having a small but important folio of "favorites," remembered in great detail and revisited. So often design seems also to rely on a sequence of random observations of situation, material, condition, on a series of almost disconnected conversations that remain in the mind as one draws.

This suggests that an important concern is *material* and that one feels more and more aware of the materiality of buildings. Increasingly irritated by diagrammatic objects, by geometric or analytical self-satisfaction. Bored by bland flanks. Jaded by the neat cut of the perfect shadow across the "art" photograph. Materiality has of course become a fashionable discussion, and no doubt there are some overly self-conscious details created in homage to Carlo Scarpa or with fond memories of the antique that can irritate . . . and will undoubtedly seem tedious to the next generation of architects. Yet materiality can be involved with the fascination in what a material can *do*. How one can invent with it. How one can fashion it. How one can get a drawing to suggest strength, tactility, lightness, fragility, or the "just-so"—implying that these qualities could be developed in the actual building itself.

Looking back over projects with which I have been involved, I can recall several sequences in which an initial degree of abstraction progressively focuses on the possibility of making "arrangments" of parts and further focuses on a state where imaginable and quite physical objects emerge.

Unintentionally a line runs from one piece of work to the next, and fascinations are sustained. Details recur. It is difficult to chronicle precisely the development of one idea—superficial thoughts remain dormant, sometimes for years, then resurface with surprising vigor under unlikely circumstances.

I have always been fascinated by the idea of ambivalent space. Indeed, the whole issue of spatial definition is central to architecture. A compelling paradox surrounds the question: What is a boundary? Are we too hidebound by the traditional search for lines of enclosure? Are we territory-obsessed?

Are we not missing something in our constantly reiterated practices of definition, of seeking typologies and models?

What is an edge? Does it necessarily demand a piece of hardware? Does it have to be celebrated quite so emphatically? The twentieth-century achievements of plate glass, structural glass, simulation, decay, and virtual reality challenge the tyranny of the wall. In conceptual terms, the edge can be treated as an instantly disposable or retrievable condition. Edges defined only while they serve to steady an understanding of overlaid territories or thoughts.

How is all this defined in nature? Surely by an incredibly rich and subtle intermingling: the time factors of mutation and growth and decay, the myriad physical forms, with winding, sheltering elements. I am not referring to any direct extrapolation of vegetable or anthropomorphic form: this is more a summary of conceptual conditions. It is these that one must contemplate when arrested by the narrowness of so much architecture.

So how might one transpose natural examples of physical (and temporal) of definition into architecture? In some ways it is left to us to find unexplored territories: not simply formally or technically but conceptually, to associate the hitherto unlikely with the likely: to use one's imagination to pursue analogies, the onset of autumn or the space occupied by moving wings—the one concerned with dynamic and temporality, the other with dynamic and spatiality. In the light of such pursuit, our architectural devices and practices look turgid.

It may be that the questioning of these assumptions only serves to clarify and eventually redefine architecture's motivational structure. Somehow, though, motive and form have become locked, with form the more narrowly interpreted of the two.

If one challenges the traditional concept of enclosure, one passes along the series of its handmaidens—walls, floors, ceilings, and the like—increasingly unsatisfied. It is one thing to believe that all has not yet been said in the playing out of their potential; it is another to ask whether our adherence to them as models actually gets in the way of responding appropriately to human need or human imagination.

In particular, one can challenge the normally performed niceties that result in the predetermined geometry of a room. If the definition of room is notionally eliminated, there is an immediate danger of erecting an alternative set of parameters that might be equally hidebound. So many times the geometry of the "room" is the result of habit, of such things as inherited ritual and questionable tradition, so that the contemporary condition has to fit into spaces generated by early twentieth-century manners, nineteenth-century protocol, and eighteenth-century aesthetics. If the television set replaces the hearth, wall-to-wall sound may simply be the precursor of the house with *no* walls. Can architecture not posit the notion of ultimate casualness in order to redeploy such elements?

In material terms, this leads to questioning what surfaces need to be (or could be) solid or continuous or transparent. Here I must confess a personal preference. I cannot deny a taste for the overlaid and the incised: translucency as well as total transparency. I believe that architecture can present a more subtle and more delightfully ambiguous face than it has.

Can the norms themselves be interchanged? Can there not be a system of architectural definition that is far more fluent and that allows the extension of logical conditions—the floor becoming the wall, if it wants to? The room defined under certain conditions, by family consensus? The wall or skin of the building giving a view out to a real prospect, or sometimes to a virtually real prospect, or to a completely simulated prospect (even, from time to time, a deadeningly negative blank wall!)?

In all of this, I remain most comfortable investigating via the drawn line. Suitably frustrated by its simplicity, I am also pleased by its relative acceptance as a shorthand. Conversations can be illustrated almost as fast as you can think by using a scribble. But does the line represent enclosure or surface? How does it deal with something that is reflected or is immaterial, a shadow? How does it deal with force and strength? How does it deal with that which hovers, threatens, glides, or melts? Perhaps this explains why alternative media are sometimes employed: bringing, as they do, a deliberate softening of pictorial territory.

In parallel, one is suspicious of the dependence upon angular geometry: the relationships between elements can surely allow distortion, particularly those that start off by being rectilinear. Instinctively, one leans on the figuration. Sometimes one keeps the figure as a distorted rectangle; sometimes one moves around the rectangle with a deliberately "bowed" line. On other occasions, there is a fracturing of the all-too-complete figuration. If all of this sounds like mere formalist play, I must reiterate my position regarding material. These lines and figures are made up (at least in the mind) of material objects: real strands and real paths. Instinctively there is some delight in suggesting something is stretched and twisted.

Several early projects pursue these questions. A very early and fairly simple example is a drawing (1976) that explores the beginnings of a fascination with artificial light. A series of depressions in the floor—a kind of "nonfurniture"—is part of a composition involving translucent screens illuminated at different levels of intensity. A complementary system of illuminated tubes rotate from horizontal to vertical and sometimes erupt into more organic forms at the edges. Looking at it now the tubes are somewhat inconsistent, but the first attempts to break out of the world of the flat and hard and constant had been made. Two or three years later, certain projects used perforated screens or meshes: all types of meshed materials, fences, and woven forms, and inevitably, the condition of the mesh as both there and not there, a marker and definer that nonetheless permits the space to flow. Layers of mesh can create a situation by which various different moments—or degrees of overlay—can simultaneously be considered as the defining condition. The wall itself is being challenged.

The first mesh discussion came about during the design of the Trondheim Library, and it was at that time but one of a set of devices used in this large building that attempted to fragment a series of institutional departments into a collection of special and concealed places sited around a large theatrical space. The mesh in this instance concerns stacking, segregating, hanging, and screening. The later meshes, such as those used in a project called Meshed Ground, act both as monitors and filters while counterbalancing (in substantive terms) the rocky and riddled ground below.

At the back of one's mind is the paradox of challenging the existing vocabulary of wall, floor, top, bottom while at the same time simply extruding and, to some extent, interweaving traditional horizontal and vertical surfaces. A mesh may simply be considered as a modulated frame, and the whole process of definition and modulation a calculated mathematical process. Yet, if we exercise another set of instincts and observations, twentieth-century cinema and screen-based technologies have given us an experience of undefined space as well as undefined time. The layers are inevitably part of that inheritance.

Meshed Ground. 1975. Project. Perspective. Airbrush, wax crayon and ink on TTS print.

The two projects—Trondheim Library and Meshed Ground—remain primarily concerned with architectural formalism and consistent geometries, and the drawings themselves remain bedded in the mid-twentieth-century mode of line perspective: the sticks, strips, and changes of direction are clearly articulated. Herein is an obvious paradox: when the intention is to distort, to extend, and to some extent to dismantle, one is still reliant upon a medium devised to *establish* and to define.

These ideas could have been developed scientifically and empirically, and this (perhaps for another designer) would be a logical approach, but one uses what one knows in the first instance. So they were crude beginnings in the pursuit of light and shadow, of creating not only an ambience but space itself.

A number of related issues are worth pursuing individually (though they inevitably lead from one to the other), but whether they constitute a *vocabulary* is another question. The first is light and shadow. Though much modern architecture lays claim to a clarity of thought in this area, the exploration of shadow was probably better understood in certain Gothic and baroque instances. Modernism might be said to have simplified the pursuit. Inevitably one can be accused of theatricalism if one waxes too lyrical about the effect of layering within the shadow, yet without some means of entry into this question one is condemned to remain incarcerated in a bland, pure, elemental territory.

I have already touched upon the *definition* of territory: we inherit the categories that insist on boundaries from both classical and modernist architecture. Despite this legacy, I find myself searching for a means by which the issue of definition could be more readily modified or even subsumed: available as a generator but by no means mandatory to the business of design.

This brings us to the question of the tangible and the intangible object. Drawing does enable you to hold certain images in a kind of no-man's-land between presence and nonpresence. Some things might move or melt or simply be shadows, hence the starting point of the Shadow House project: full frontality, the definitely-there object, and the extant condition are being challenged. Certain parts of the scheme were placed in such a way as to create shadows towards the approaching inhabitant, or cast shadows on other elements, themselves often membranes and meshes.

The complementary idea of *suggested* space and the suggested image arises. Certain architectural theorists have pursued the question of allusion: the suggested reference. Here I am closer to the tactic of illusion, more pictorial than literal. Yet the intention is to provoke thought and momentary consideration of that which confronts you, rather than just making an architecture of named (and overnamed) parts. The announcement of space has traditionally followed the habit of identifying elements, establishing hierarchies, or creating predictable sequences. In an architecture of shadows, light, and filters, there may well be an ambiguity of defined *space* or *place*.

An *ephemeral* space may well be the goal. In ephemeral space, it is the moment that establishes its role or its relevance. This may shift in prominence or in physical definition, in overtness or apparent presence: its role may increase or diminish vis-à-vis other parts of the building. It may not even be there the next day, or it may only be appreciated at certain times of the day or from a certain direction.

It is important that one observes light as essentially mobile. It can be filtered, captured, and almost "hauled" into a building, even within the niceties of hard, rational architecture. In harness with an architecture that delights in ambiguity and illusion, light can be used as a counterpoint to the softer conditions, or, alternatively, as a source of further contrivance.

Ideally, one would like to think of a vocabulary of methods as being open-ended. It would be arch to think of a completely self-sufficient language. If the tradition of the window (as well as that of the clerestory and the roof light) as aperture has its limits and can now be challenged by exploiting elec-

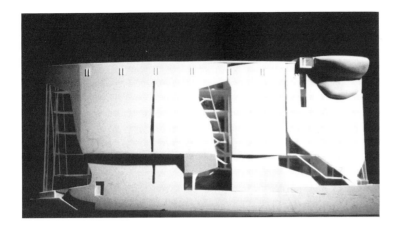

tronics, then surely electronic techniques can also be laid end-to-end with the window tradition.

We designed a series of solar houses for the town of Landstuhl in the Rhineland Palatinate. One of these was very nearly built: a blue house with a semicircular southern flank. It was our first experience of working within quite explicit rules of both active and passive solar design. In the end the decisions to expose parts of the building or shield them from the sun arose quite directly. The effort to create apertures became much more deliberate, and the pathways of both heat and light emerged as an essential component rather than as the result of applied aesthetics. To some extent the Shadow House project was contrived as a reaction to the pragmatism of the solar houses, a necessary reminder that deliberateness is not the whole issue.

For one is constantly moving in and out of a position that could be justified to the most correct of one's academic colleagues; on the other hand, refusing to believe that some kind of alchemy is impossible in a world that has already accepted smart glass and dynamic structures. My approach is quite unrhetorical; I prefer to track around the materials and phenomena that I have experienced, particularly those that are visual.

If we observe water we are in the presence of a substance that has volume, power, reflectivity, and trajectory *but no color*, and thus it is an ideal support for illusionary manipulations. Furthermore, water creates sound, which in confined spaces tends to be identifiable with but also subject to a certain theatricality. A project for Porchester Baths was produced simultaneously with projects by my students—a dangerous thing to do, perhaps—but there was no fear that we would employ the same gambits. The opportunity to combine the qualities of water and glass, fast and slow liquid, with their passing singular and contrary qualities was intriguing. The notion of steam as an architectural condition and the translucency of steam with its potential for illusion were used to pursue the possibility of ambivalent boundaries.

The ambivalent boundary appears in another medium within this project as reiterated structure. Approached obliquely, its lines seem to disappear, then at another angle they reassert themselves. Once again, it is a territory that can be incorporated into the architecture of shadows, light, and filters.

Projects of the last few years share another physical consistency through the device of the "path" or primary circulatory route. Even in the work of the 1970s, such as the Trondheim Library, an arcaded path acts as a reference to the whole undulating space. A project for the Japanese Shinkenchiku competition was called the Via Appia House; a dramatic contrast was made between two intersecting paths (the subject, determined and judged by Richard Meier, was that of "a house at an intersection"). One path leads upward, flanked by shiny, clear surfaces, and ends on a celebratory platform with dramatic views. The other path delves down into a mysterious chamber in the ground, flanked by rusticated and overgrown surfaces.

In other works, there has been a less direct interpretation. Paths need not be what they seem. They can, as in the competition project for the Akademie Für Bildende und Kunst in Frankfurt, act as the common denominator of a widely varied set of circumstances: passing nonchalantly by, as it were, with the cut and thrust of the spaces and events using the path only as a referencing condition and not as a galvanizing force. Half of the building was an existing Carmelite church, and the rest was new. In this case the path is a perambulation that sets up a series of views toward the old and new spaces and toward some exhibition set pieces. Distanced referencing is, after all, the familiar condition of the "scenic route" and of almost any relationship perceived from a railway, road, or flight path.

The aesthetic of the weaving path is tempting: if it can result from ambiguous relationships among several routes, then we have the embryonic architecture in which line becomes sympathetic to the shading and filtering already discussed. If the line implies a journey, it can also unravel a narrative. There might be revelation or surprise. (More recently, our *yatai* at Nagoya and folly at the Osaka Expo synthesize ideas to do with transparencies, masks, blurred definitions, and threaded spiral routes.)

Design of the first substantial building, Social Housing at Luetzoplatz in Berlin, began in the mid-eighties and was completed in 1990. The prolonged gestation period, the result of a volatile political and economic climate, allowed the luxury of returning to and developing the preoccupations of the previous ten years. This building has two distinct characters: the veiled, Gothic, and slightly theatrical public face and the parody of Teutonic austerity on its private face. Internally the spaces reflect the need to seek out as much light and openness as possible, to obscure the dictated and oppressively small spaces. Vertical shafts are carved out and expressed externally; walls tilt and splay to allow maximum light to penetrate. The outer winter gardens offer a spidery enclosure in which to watch the life of Luetzoplatz, an extension of the main living space and a veil that casts its own shadowing impression on the interior.

During the long period of developing the Berlin housing, we worked on a number of competitions, most based in Germany and most highly prescriptive—the degree of prescription in much of the work was quite breathtaking. One sensed that the authors of the competition briefs wanted schemes of a particular sort because that was how it had always been done. In response to what I felt was an increasingly limited arena in which to work, I embarked on an experiment in methodology (Peckham Housing) that unfortunately failed, but the experience provided several moments of reflection. The project looked at a decayed area of South London and in particular observed its material context. Contextual reference is a mechanical and clichéd gesture that conventionally ignores both the cultural and subcultural evidence of a contemporary community. Contextual references are most easily made to and through the physical edifices of the past.

I was more interested in the idea of cyclical change, of deformed evidence of transient states. The chosen area and site are full of ill-regarded remnants, of crumbling walls, of bits of rusted and scorched metal fence. Graffiti and layered shreds of posters tell of events both violent and entertaining. Yet the metamorphosis is not entirely negative; the physical evidence tells of a culture not sustained through money and preservation but through spirit. There is the visual appeal of the patina as well as of the deformations, but also the more philosophical appeal of cyclical change and the possibility of reinterpreting these elements. The project not only occupies the same site as these fragments but borrows from them both aesthetically and literally. Once again the idea of the room as a box dissolves, as do the classical rules of hierarchy.

Social Housing, Lützoplatz, Berlin.
1988–89. Front elevation

Social Housing, Lützoplatz. Interior

a. Peckham Housing, London, U.K.
1990. Project. Ground floor imprint

b. First-level plan

c. Mid-level plan

d. Prototypical wall

e. Interior view

More recently we have been involved in designing a narrative that tests invisible connections in a project that will be built: a sequence of buildings and structures stretched across the Austrian landscape close to the spa town of Bad Deutsch-Altenburg. The project is concerned with making connections with the past in the form of a small museum to house the relics of the nearby Roman settlement of Carnuntum, an exhibition pavilion that chronicles the history of the area, an amphitheater that provides a facility for local theater, and a belvedere sited on a remote quarried edge that allows one to survey the panoramic national borders. All parts weave an interlocked story about the past, the present, and the future. Spatial ambiguities are declared first with the museum, whose contents are placed outside the building; with the pavilion, whose ground is also a roof; and with the belvedere, which articulates the language of the buildings that stand before it in the landscape.

For the last few years I have taken responsibility for two schools of architecture: the University of East London and more recently the Bartlett, University College London. It is an oddly balanced world, that of teaching, of administration, and of running a small practice. There are obviously implicit areas of overlap, but how one's own thoughts crop up in conversations with students, the relationship between designing and teaching, has to be unraveled. Certainly teaching offers a more *self-conscious* area in which to debate ideas than elsewhere. Consciously or unconsciously one discloses one's own preoccupations in what passes for objective criticism: this is inevitable if one is not just an uninvolved cipher. There is in fact a kind of weaving process in which a project is implicitly criticized—in both directions. Conversely, a succinct line of tutorial judgment might challenge one's own work. The trick is to keep one's judgment and that of the student sufficiently distanced and thus to sustain the creativity of all concerned. How often has one watched the ideas of a talented designer gradually atrophy as he or she becomes too intense a critic. I can therefore admit to a certain self-preserving hypocrisy on occasion.

How much one's own attitudes are imposed on the students I'm not sure. I suspect that they get suspended in favor of some line of encouragement of *their* process. Similarly, I'm not too worried if a good building arrives via a set of values different from my own. Another by-product of teaching is the filtration of ideas that arise more or less contemporaneously with one's own work. Schools of architecture generate a useful "slippage" whereby the aptness, adventurousness, or precision of offered thoughts is quite uneven.

You can then (mentally) offer your own ideas on whichever pieces of architectural culture might be useful. Or is this all an idealization of the relationship between teaching and practice? I hear myself (and others) mouth that the balance between theoretical ideology and practical involvement is ideal. It is of course ideal—but does it really happen?

Is not the world in which ideas and their pursuit are surely valued one which is unsullied by economic pressures or clients who wish to compromise? In school there is the constant pursuit of a truth—or at least of a certain type of consistent thought. The teacher-architect may sometimes be relieved of the pressure to make her practice a commercial success. A luxury, or a short-lived buffer?

In truth, the academic scene in Britain is inflexible and overly bureaucratic. Burgeoning pressures are now placed on academics that threaten the way in which we like to teach. Equally they threaten (because they completely ignore) the subtlety and quality of relationships by which one runs an architecture school. Bureaucratic tidiness is pursued in a pedantic and time-consuming way. Little national value is placed on excellence, specialness, wit, or creativity—particularly in any territory related to the visual arts. If you run a school of architecture, as I do, your worth is measured by whether the school is cost-effective or satisfies the templated standards (imagine yourself being templated—robotized—homogenized?). "And do we attract *precisely* the right number of students?" they ask. So we create smoke screens and protective barriers for our (eccentric and fragile) colleagues, a sleight of hand by which we quantify the unquantifiable and justify that which needs no justification.

From time to time one becomes the shrill advocate or defender of work that *in no way* represents one's own position but is still work that should be pursued. Just as there is no normative description of good architecture, there is no single path toward its creation. In a school one must be concerned with creativity, and there never seems to be enough time fully to elucidate it.

In an office one must be concerned with maintaining creativity, and there never seems to be enough time for that either: the real, the unreal world, the ordered and the inspirational, it is all there but I am not sure that I can balance it properly or make sense of what I have—but maybe that is part of the intrigue.

a. Pfaffenberg Competition, Bad
Deutsch/Altenburg. 1992. Carnuntum
Museum and display cabinet detail

b. Exhibition pavilion in the landscape

c. Belvedere. Plan

d. Belvedere. Section and perspective

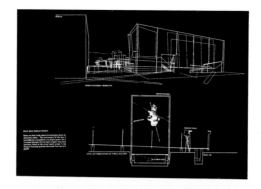

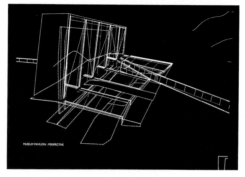

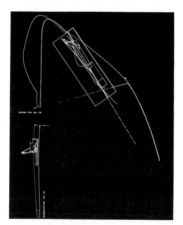

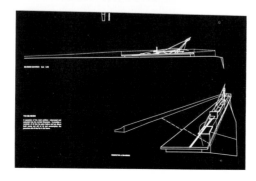

a. Pfaffenberg Competition. Exhibition pavilion. Model.

b. Exhibition auditoriums. Model.

c. Belvedere. Model.

Chapter 9

PROJECTS / RECOLLECTIONS   Merrill Elam

Preface:

Each of the following vignettes concerns a single project. Simultaneously, each vignette contains (a) recollection(s), not necessarily or directly associated with the illustrated project.

While the marginal texts describe the projects, the recollections, which have been collected from a number of people over a period of time, indicate areas of interest, moments of observation retained, and personal inclinations.

As disjointed and varied as they may appear/seem/read, they inform the collective consciousness of those who have gathered together to labor over the projects.

These pages, the models, the recollections, and the drawings conspire to lend insights into a particular way of making/thinking.

The High Museum at the Georgia Pacific Center Atlanta, Georgia, 1986. This public art museum is installed in an existing corporate office tower in downtown Atlanta, Georgia.

The space provided is within a greenhouse structure approximately 24 feet wide by 140 feet long by 40 feet tall, at the rear of the main lobby behind an auditorium. The long dimension faces directly south gaining day-long exposure to sunlight.

The program includes approximately 5,000 square feet of gallery (750 running feet of display surface), administrative offices, museum shop, art preparation, receiving and shipping, and circulation, a total of 12,000 square feet.

The museum is a building within a building. Classical elements of architectural composition (procession, facade, entry, symbolic space, and program) were reconfigured and rearranged to adapt to the existing conditions.

The primary images of the museum architecture are established by the ramp system and the vaulted structure of the upper gallery. The composition equally distributes the ramp and the upper gallery about the entrance-lobby axis, a bisecting line formed by the relationship of the auditorium to the tower lobby. The symmetrical plan generates asymmetrical composition in the third dimension, with the upper gallery, a solid element, juxtaposed with the openness of the ramp. Circulation via the ramp takes one down to the first gallery, which occurs on an intermediate level. The ramp allows patrons to move both vertically and horizontally through the space, with views to the interior as well as out to the cityscape. After the first gallery level, the ramp continues to the lower level, where the largest galleries and loading docks are located. Portions of the space extend the full three stories, allowing the display of very large sculptures.

The room was too large, a contemporary effort at grandness. The beds were dwarfed, but the space was cool and light-colored. The room was rectilinear with the long axis to the beach and the Adriatic; and the window affording that view was at once ordinary and extraordinary. It was flush with the skin of the building, and tall almost to the ceiling and opened inward—two wood frames with large glass panels. A ledge and rail protruded only a few inches from the building's surface, not quite comfortable for sitting but irresistible. Inside, curtains hung from ceiling to floor, parting in the center in layers and making a small fabric-enclosed room just at the window, a window-room, a magic zone of inside and outside.

At night, wrapped in that secret tiny space, it was easy to own the darkness of the Adriatic and the moon and the space of both: to become a nocturnal Pegasus.

m.e.

Willie said, "yes sir . . . this building is special, this building has a concept." He said, "Just go out there at the street and walk right down there, through the middle, all the way to the window down there, and yes sir, something happens to you . . . yes sir, this building has a concept."

Willie the worker to m.s.

There are only two things that can't be welded: the crack of dawn and a broken heart.

worker to m.s.

It was not until we were out of the red Porsche, inside and down the stairs, that we realized that the concrete was soft, touchable, like a comforter or eiderdown. Glass, low down and horizontal, proclaimed the walls weightless. The enclosure was an incredible inversion of materials, a rewriting of their very natures.

m.e. to m.s. at the Koshino House

Criss built this thing alongside the expressway. How bizarre—not really of the landscape yet not far enough removed to be a comment on or critique of the landscape. Maybe it was lack of definition, difference, and separation that caused the tension, the fascination, the frustration.

m.e.: critique of Criss Mill's landscape installation

Radio Station Headquarters WQXI AM/FM Atlanta, Georgia, 1985. Located in Atlanta, Georgia, this is the 34,000-square-foot headquarters and radio broadcast facility of WQXI-94Q, a subsidiary of Jefferson Pilots Communications Company. The station's long-run success as one of the nation's top popular music stations is the result of on-air programming versatility and, in large measure, the vitality and exuberance of the management and staff. On one hand is the all-energy, twenty-four-hour-a-day, good-humor, high-spirit, and razzle-dazzle on-the-air emporium; on the other is the stable, bottom-line oriented, fiercely competitive, highly lucrative business. The client wanted to build a new facility, more than twice the size of that existing, that would embody and, to the greatest degree possible, amplify the unique qualities of the station's corporate culture and public image.

Plan and section relationships encourage the high-energy, crisscrossing activities and interaction of the staff. Intersections, nodes, two-way stairs, extra stairs, balconies, transparencies, and remotely located interdependent functions are the architectural devices. The collage of the organization plan derives from responses to the site edge conditions and the program; its geometry directly relates to the antenna's position within the plan field.

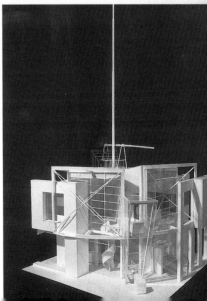

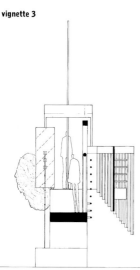

In the pool, belly down like a giant frog, at eye level with the river and the marshes, it is easy to be one with nature, to be an intimate and necessary part of that sensuous sultry landscape. Above, up the slope on an emerald green plateau, stitching the border between jungle and cultivated lawn, sits a poetic redefinition of the rational grid of the Enlightenment and the Southern plantation. It confirms once and always that poetic and formal ideas of past eras can be absolutely evoked and expanded by sensitive reinterpretation and reconfiguration.

m.e. at Middleton Inn

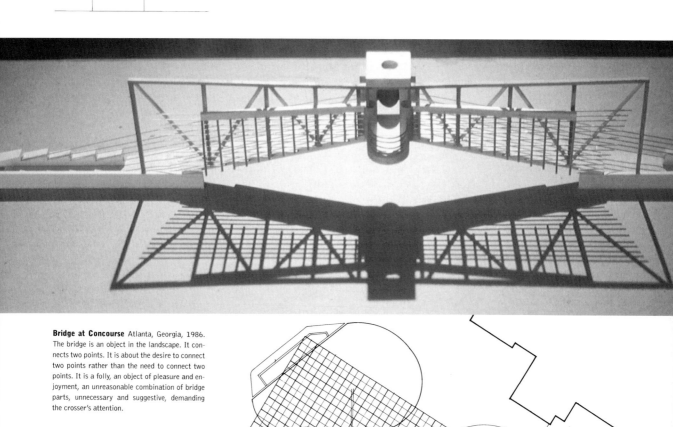

Bridge at Concourse Atlanta, Georgia, 1986. The bridge is an object in the landscape. It connects two points. It is about the desire to connect two points rather than the need to connect two points. It is a folly, an object of pleasure and enjoyment, an unreasonable combination of bridge parts, unnecessary and suggestive, demanding the crosser's attention.

They had walked to the piazza, to the Trevi Fountain, students at the American Academy, in continuing debate, absorbing every architectural move within their capacities to absorb. It was late, after the evening meal and wine, and a light had entered the city. The naked lamp suspended like an eye overhead on its electric wires was caught in the air, making and remaking the architecture. It was Kahn who could not leave the piazza.

   m.e.: a story told by Joe Amisano

It was the underside of a very white mushroom, light incredibly reflecting from unknown sources and tiny views between the blades of grass out to the pastoral landscape. It was structural somehow from a radiating central point, yet noninsistent. The mushroom had been chopped or severed so that it was actually only half the mushroom. The half that survived wanted only to be light and not a building at all. The first hint was the nonstatement of the entrance facade: grey, minimal, existing out of necessity. The facade, on that monastic campus, was enigmatic and ill-placed in terms of contextual effort. The interior, the mushroom underside, was ephemeral, a cloud of light and nonmaterial.

   m.e.: Aalto's library at Mount Angel

Atlanta Chamber of Commerce Atlanta, Georgia, 1987. The Atlanta Chamber of Commerce building is a 28,000-square-foot office, reception, and conference facility.

The building is a ship anchored in a river of traffic. Inside, looking out, one has the sense of a constant current flowing past or of the structure itself calmly moving upstream. The prow or front of the building bends slightly with the force of the current. The building is located on a triangle circumscribed by streets, and the riverlike movement results from this happenstance of site.

As in many flatiron buildings of the 1920s, the plan form of the Chamber is generated from the site. Building walls hug property and set-back lines in an attempt to gain the maximum floor area.

The Chamber is adjacent to the internalized, mega-sized Omni complex on one side, sprawling parking lots and nondescript one- and two-story light-industrial buildings on the others. Although located in downtown Atlanta, the site is not on the Peachtree Street corridor and is therefore out of the mainstream. To counter the neighborhood, to pin the building to the triangular site, and to give the Chamber presence, we incorporated a slightly exaggerated cupola. Future administrations may choose to use this as an observation room. The cupola, beyond relating to the context, reflects the clients' desire for an image that spoke to "the traditions of the City and the dynamics of the phoenix rising from the ashes." In other words, the cupola, a traditional form in southern architecture, is reintroduced sleek and stylized. It also responds to the continuing desire in the City's personality for formality.

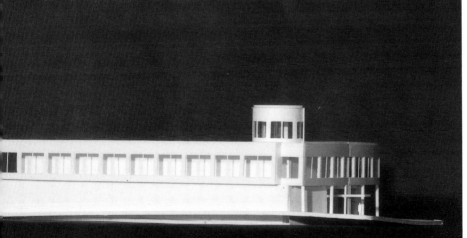

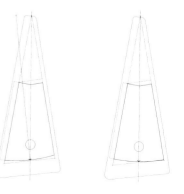

On the edge of the drafting surface was a small collection of paper shards fixed together, no larger than a medium-sized thumbnail. It contained an entire thesis.

m.e.

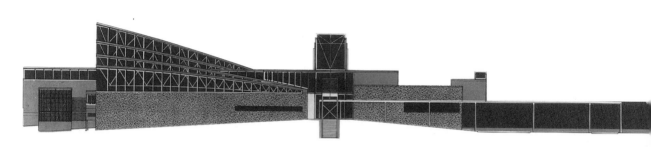

Clayton County Headquarters Library Jonesboro, Georgia, 1986. Jonesboro, Georgia, is wedged in between the southeast end of Hartsfield International Airport, one of the busiest airports in the world, and Tara, the mythical home of Scarlet O'Hara. The strip between the two is folksy, hand-painted (not at all mass-produced), a place where one is apt to pull alongside a pickup with a rack and ZZ Top coming at you through the open windows. It is a place where information is sought for practical reasons and history is personal. Scholars will not seek out obscure dissertation-supporting materials here. This library is more a filling station for information for living life: a puppet show, a cooking class, a seed catalogue . . . Easy parking. Come on in. A K-Mart for information . . .

Where the tree fell, an opening occurred in the woods. The house occupies the position of the fallen tree. The house also occupies the attitude of the people who inhabit it: an attitude of multiplicities and dualities. The house is firmly planted on the ground but rises above it. The interior spaces enclose and protect and, at the same time, imply extensions into the space of the woods. Particular exterior zones are one with particular interior zones. The house is narrow but not limited. It is isolated in the woods yet at its very heart is the *goshinden* room, in which light and companionship are shared.

Chmar House

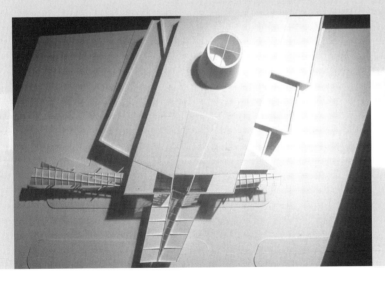

Buckhead Branch Library Atlanta, Georgia, 1989. The site is atop a crest that commands a view of downtown Atlanta. The new building consumes the large narrow portion of the site in between the distant frontages, perched in full view of downtown. An array of canopies intensifies the pedestrian scale along Buckhead Avenue and deposits the viewer at the helm of the spectator city, air-conditioned and detached.

This 22,000-square-foot neighborhood library is located in a unique nouveau riche strip of Atlanta. The Buckhead neighborhood is the forefront of an ethnic shift in which the boutique replaces the pool hall. The neighborhood is a rupture, showing signs of a downtown with growing pains.

The existing Ida Williams Branch is a parking meter past expired, unable to communicate with speed and clarity. Today's public library is a locus for knowledge within a civic landscape bounded by mobile sprawl and strip shopping.

Turner Village at the Candler School of Theology, Emory University Atlanta, Georgia, 1989. Turner Village, at the northern edge of the expanding Emory University campus, is a discrete compound of housing, community center, and chapel for theology students, visiting lecturers, and transient missionaries. Dialogue and interaction among the various village occupants was the desired objective.

The architectural program included renovation of thirteen apartment buildings and construction of a new community center of 14,000 square feet and a small chapel.

The site, a one-acre horse pasture threatened by mini-warehouses, is adjacent to a fried chicken establishment, a drive-up dry cleaner's, a strip shopping center, and mid-sized suburban dream homes. The only predictable view is up . . . to the clouds through the pines.

Even the earth is a stratum of transition, fill left over from twenty years of recent construction. It is a zone of uneasy juncture of farmland and suburban sprawl.

m.e.: *Carol Cobb, Turner Branch Library*

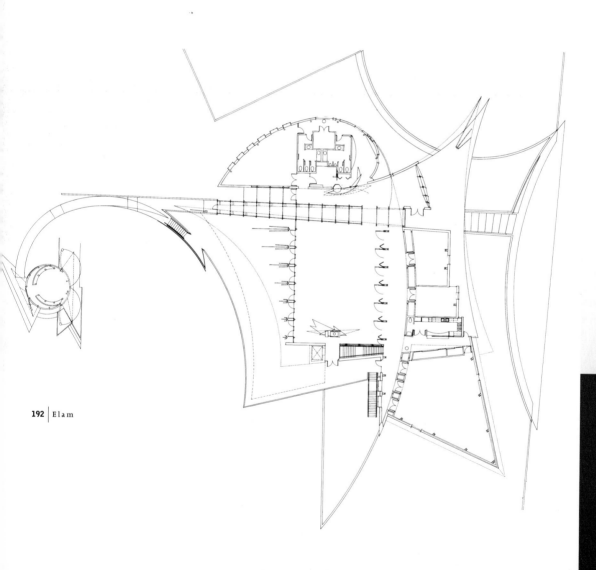

4 1/2" aluminum storefront
steel plate column
edge of steel grating above
2 × 2 × 1/4" steel-tube ribs
6" pipe column
1/4" curved acrylic canopy
canopy steel frame
screen-wall steel frame
poured-in-place concrete wall
C6 × 8.2 steel channel w/1/4" steel plate cover
conc. curb
intermediate steel beam cut from @ 10 × 45
1 1/2" corrugated metal roofing, 18 ga. w/end closures
1/4" steel cover plate
12 ga.-formed metal frame
laminated safety glass w/(2) pieces 3/16" heat-
strengthened glass w/.060 interlayment
5" × 12" steel column w/(2) C12 × 25 steel channels; weld
& grind smooth
C6 × 8.2 steel channel w/1/4" steel plate cover
3/4" exterior plywd soffit
outline of screen wall forward of section
C9 × 13.4 steel channel
3" pipe column welded to steel channel; align bottom of
tube w/bottom of steel channel
2 × 2 × 1/4" steel tube
1/4" curved acrylic canopy w/20' radius
canopy steel frame w/(2) C9 × 15 steel channels; weld &
grind smooth
projected line of canopy frame
4" pipe column, typ.
steel frame—1/4" steel plate
steel frame—(2) C12 × 25 steel channels; weld & grind smooth
1 1/2" × 1" steel channel welded to round bar or steel
frame; bolt thru channel & glazing @ quarter points
(2) 4 × 5.4 steel channels; weld & grind smooth
structural silicone sealant
1/4" polycarbonate glazing w/eased edges, bottom & sides
(2) 3/4" Ø round bars
(2) 3/4" × 3" flat bars
(2) 1/2" Ø round bars
poured in place conc. wall

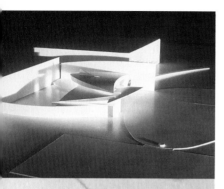

Proposal for an Entry Building—Herman Miller Main Site Zeeland, Michigan, 1987. Attached to more than one million square feet of office, manufacturing, and distribution facilities, the entry building is little more than a pavilion, an introduction to the spine that connects a campus of separate structures.

Programmatically, the entry building is two rooms: a reception room and a living room. Supplemental areas include toilets, coatroom, luggage storage, and a small office for guests.

The sequence of events is classical in function: arrival, reception, progression, arrival, pause, decision, progression. The architectural forms enhance each event but collectively form a whole. While the models and drawings of the entry building are slick and clean, the intent was to make an architecturally "strokable" building, textured and finely detailed. Materials and forms are inseparable in content and presentation.

She asked, "Is this the house of the future?"

Before I could reply she said, "This is the house of the future . . . where the spirit soars and the feet stay on the ground . . . You can have your cake and eat it too: you can be on land and space at the same time in the same house . . . The house of the future has your mind in space and your feet on the ground."

She continued, "It ain't gonna work with their mind down here . . . the house of the future . . . The people in the future wanna have their feet in civilization—in old traditions and want their spirits to soar into space . . . All in one area they want both feelings; they want their feet on the ground and their spirits up there where other people can't mess with it . . . They wanna be isolated, but they don't wanna to be totally isolated . . . They want to be isolated, but when they want to be with other people, they want it instantly . . . They want it instantly where they can step down two steps and be there immediately . . . two steps down to reality."

I asked her if she understood the drawings, and she said (with tears in her eyes), "The average person won't understand these drawings," but she could . . . "People with vision will understand these drawings."

Susan's mother's reactions to the plans for the Chmar house. Sunday 4/16/89

I raced motorcycles; now I race architecture.

m.s. to m.e.

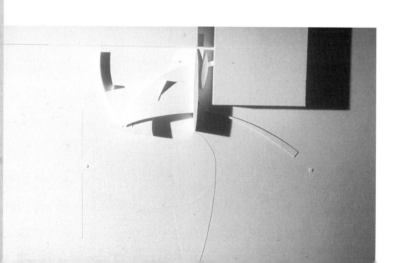

The museum was unlike any other place/space that Susan had ever experienced, at once traditional and rational and also unworldly. The people were busts, the busts people. Light was everywhere from nowhere. Susan in wonderland.

impressions from Susan's slides of the Glyptotek: m.e. in response

In some places in the South, for a short period in warm weather in the woods after dark, an architecture of sound and light emerges. A reverse meteor shower; the lightning bugs rise from the grasses making a blinking, deep fabric of darkness and fluorescent sequins. The tree-frog symphony fills in all of the spaces of darkness between the blinks.

m.e.

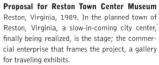

Proposal for Reston Town Center Museum
Reston, Virginia, 1989. In the planned town of Reston, Virginia, a slow-in-coming city center, finally being realized, is the stage; the commercial enterprise that frames the project, a gallery for traveling exhibits.

Just as the gallery program contrasts and complements the commercial program of the city center, the gallery architecture (delicate and airborne) contrasts and complements that of the city center (massive and earthbound). At the principal crossing of the city center's formal orthogonal axis is an opening, a sliver of land 250 feet long by 120 feet wide. Here the gallery, a gift of and for the arts and culture, is to reside.

The exhibition spaces are located on the upper level; the entry, lobby, gift shop, art handling, and cafe on the ground level. The two levels are connected by a glass-enclosed ramp, an urban observatory. The city center's orthogonal order informs the gallery's plan and orders the disposition of architectural elements: the sphere-dome, the central axis, the observation window.

Materials include a structural steel frame, copper sheathing, and glass.

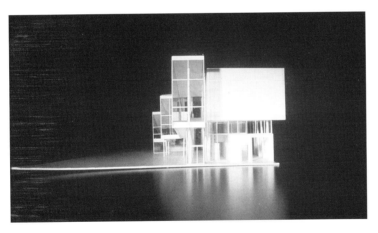

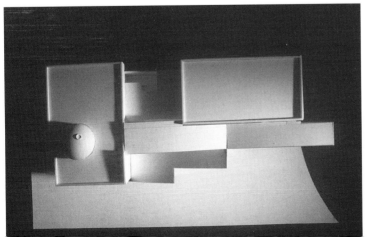

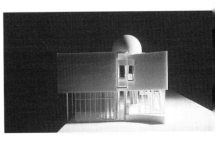

Proposal for AT&T Tallahassee Headquarters
Tallahassee, Florida, 1987. The proposed AT&T
Tallahassee Headquarters is, in effect, a tiny
high-rise, unusual, even as a proposal, in today's
world of bulky towers with extremely large floor
areas; AT&T is petite.

The site, 61 feet wide and 153 feet deep, is located on the top of a hill in downtown Tallahassee. The tightness of the site, its relationship to
surrounding buildings, and its elevation are central to the development of the building design.

Five levels of parking are just above the lobby
and retail space at ground level. Automobiles access the parking via an alleyway along the east
property line and a ramp system at the north.
Seven levels of office space and two penthouse
levels are above the parking levels. The office
space and penthouse structures rise above surrounding structures, affording views of Tallahassee and the magnificent Florida countryside.

For the site to accommodate automobiles, the
ramp system projects over the alleyway. The
power and rotational motion of automobiles on
the ramp energize the scheme and generated the
building's form.

A T-shirt-tight skin of glass and masonry is
laid over the building, taut and revealing.

The door closed behind them at the hand of a stranger. In the abandoned jail,
imprisoned—involuntarily and off guard, and even only for a few minutes, the
finality and power of that enclosure overtook every minute element of their
persons; horrifying and defeating, it was the physical realization of imprison-
ment, loss of freedom, and total loss of self-direction. All things became more
precious instantaneously.

l.b. in New Orleans: as told to m.e.

The campus and spine,
designed by Charles Eames, Quincy Jones, George Nelson, and
other notable architects, form an elegant, well-mannered
modernist collection.
The entry building is a respectful counterpoint.
Its sculptural planes and surfaces, actual and implied,
glide and slide with respect to one another,
forming spaces
that hold and nurture
but only instantaneously.
The experience of the entry building encourages a
heightened appreciation of its adjacent predecessors.

Proposal for an Entry Building—Herman Miller Main Site

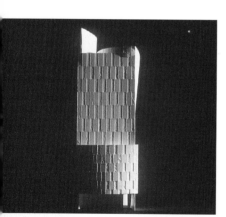

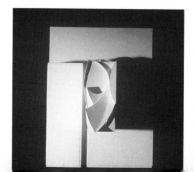

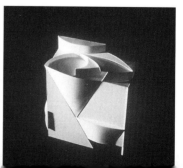

Suzi introduced me to Myron as one of the designers of the new Buckhead library.

I asked, "Have you seen it?"

He said, "You know, you got it right . . . You can do anything you want to a library just so long as you don't mess around with the Dewey Decimal system!"

a Buckhead boutique owner to s.d.

It was the pig film that got me started thinking.

m.s. to m.e.

Chmar House Atlanta, Georgia, 1989. The site is two-and-one-half acres of woods, adjacent along its longest property line to a forest, three miles from the heart of downtown Atlanta. This 4,000-square-foot house was designed for a couple anticipating children and visiting parents.

The house is a simple wood structure, clad in stucco and glass and metal roofing. The driveway is gravel.

postscript:

Architecture is inextricably lodged between the phenomenal and the deductive.

Our engagement with architecture involves more than the manipulation of a motif or of limited moves within an a priori process. It entangles three intensive pursuits: the physical, the intellectual, and the intuitive. Our physical and intellectual pursuits are strict, disciplined, difficult acts. Our intuitive pursuits move from the realm of exactitude toward an intuitive rightness. It is the search for intuitive rightness that holds our greatest fascination. The awareness of this almost inexplicable, instinctive, ironic consciousness has most clarified our intent and methods in architecture.

It is cumulative personal experience that feeds intuition and hones instinct. This realm of intuition and instinct is the mortar of the lodging: the link between the phenomenal and the deductive. It is a mortar not only of the joints but one that permeates the fabric of the whole and folds back on itself.

Chapter 10

THE RETURN OF (THE REPRESSED) NATURE

Diana Agrest

Frontispiece: Forces of Inscription,
Diana Agrest, photomontage 1992

As nature came to seem more like a machine, did not the machine come to seem more natural?"

—*Sandra Harding*[1]

This essay originated with the China Basin project, a theoretical urban proposal for San Francisco developed for the exhibition *Visionary San Francisco* held at the city's Museum of Modern Art in 1990. While being an instinctive response to the question of the American city and urbanism today, its retrospective reading led me to focus on the question of nature. Although the project preceded the text, I have reversed the order of their presentation here, thus providing a framework for the understanding of the project rather than presenting the project as an application of it.

For the past fifty years the question of nature has been conspicuously absent from urbanistic discourse. This symptomatic absence has generated the critical examination of ideology that this text represents: an exploration of the conditions that articulate and structure the notions of nature, architecture, and gender in the ideology of modernist urbanism.

The American city, a city that regulates (suppresses or generates) enjoyment through the presence of object buildings, plays a key role in the unraveling of this complex articulation, indicating the repetition of a symptom that goes back to the original (American) urban scene/sin: the violation of nature by the machine; a confrontation in which, in the struggle between the machine and the forces of nature, woman is suppressed.

Nature has been a referent for Western architectural discourse from Vitruvius through the Renaissance, when beauty, the most important property of buildings, was supposed to result from the re-presentation of nature. Only in the nineteenth century with Durand's critique of architecture as representation, was there a break with this tradition.[2] It is in the twentieth century, in Le Corbusier's *Ville contemporaine*,[3] Plan voisin, and *Ville radieuse*[4] that nature reappears in the urban discourse, not as part of an architectural metaphoric operation, but as an element in an urbanistic metonymic construct. It is not only in the European urbanistic discourse that we find clues to the absence of nature, but also in the American ideological construction of the relationship between nature and city and its articulation with the process of urbanization. The current absence of nature in urban discourse is related precisely to the suppressed relationship between European urbanistic discourse and the American city. The American city—that place where urban development directly coincides with the westward displacement of the frontier, where a rational order was applied to virgin land—presents the most pertinent example of the relationship between nature and the city in twentieth-century urbanism as ideology and its articulation with the real.[5]

The development of the American city can be explained through the opposition between nature and culture, wilderness and the city. In this equation the city was considered evil, as the place of sin, and was assigned a negative sign while nature, equated with God, embodied everything that was positive. "By the time Emerson wrote *Nature* in 1836, the terms God and Nature could be used interchangeably."[6] Ideas of God's nature and God in nature became hopelessly entangled. The moral and aesthetic qualities with which nature was imbued were considered far superior to economic and urban forces and the potential for development those forces represented. The pastoral ideal was a distinctly American theory of society and an all-embracing ideology; America was seen by Europeans as a place that, as virgin land, offered the possibility of a new beginning for an already developed Europe.[7] However, when the frontier began to be pushed westward and wilderness was to be conquered, the city, by necessity, came to be seen as a positive term, since towns were necessary in order to facilitate the development of the land; and nature, which came to represent the danger of the unknown, became the negative term. This conflict between city and country was already present in Jefferson's *Notes on Virginia*, in which he recognizes both the great political and economic potential of the machine and the fact that it will alter rural life.[8]

The machine, both product of and vehicle for the scientific revolution, made industrialization possible in a manner apparently consistent with the democratic project; at the same time, it both became and symbolized a threat to the pastoral ideal. The greatest manifestation of this conflict appears in the form of the locomotive, the machine that disturbs the peaceful rural idyll, as Nathaniel Hawthorne so vividly describes in *Sleepy Hollow*, his reaction to the process of urbanization.[9] The locomotive that slashes and scars the virgin land, is the machine that makes possible the westward conquest of the wilderness, paradoxically destroying what it wants to discover. The more nature was conquered and exploited, the more a growing consciousness of its value as wilderness developed in anticipation of its ultimate destruction. Suddenly Americans came to the realization that, as opposed to Europeans' historical past, their true past was nature itself. Extraordinary views of nature afforded by the new accessibility to the wilderness became equated with the beautiful and the sublime as defined by European Romantics; and in the arts, it was in painting that the sublime in nature was most powerfully manifested.[10] Nature was equated with

God, and painters who could portray nature as God's work, emissaries of God on earth. But paradoxically, "the new significance of nature and the development of landscape painting coincided with the relentless destruction of the wilderness into the early 19th century."[11] Thomas Cole represented this paradox in his series of paintings, *The Course of Empire—Savage State, Pastoral State, Consummation, Destruction,* and *Devastation.*[12] However, the locomotive crossing the virgin land "was like nothing seen before," and in order to reconcile the power of the machine with the beauty and peacefulness of the rural countryside, a discourse in which the power of the machine could be praised, a technological sublime, had to be developed.[13]

The mid-nineteenth century ideology of science, in which the entire universe was seen as a mechanism and the machine was viewed as part of this natural universe, provided the mediation that made the machine acceptable. However, this philosophy, in neutralizing the contradiction of accepting the machine as a positive force, facilitated the destruction of the very landscape that represented the pastoral ideal.[14]

The ideological displacements that made possible the notion of the machine as mediator in the opposition between nature and city cannot be properly understood without introducing the problematic question of nature and science, in particular as it relates to scientific discourse, considered the "mirror" of nature. But for the ideology of that discourse to be understood in its many

The Lackawana Valley, George Inness, 1855

implications, another term needs to be added: that of gender, as it relates to both nature and science.

In exploring the relationship between nature and science it is important to recognize the equivalence between nature and woman that, historically, scientific discourse has developed. Nature gendered female, has been seen in philosophy and throughout the history of science as either an organism or a mechanism.[15] According to the first view, nature was feminine and passive while husbandry, the active exploitation of nature, was masculine. Thus, the male was made essential to the cultivation of nature's latent fertility, just as in procreation, the egg was seen as passive and the sperm as active, making the male more "essential" to the process.[16] This equating of nature and female is key to understanding the struggle for power and the engendering of the parties in that struggle where power is gendered male. It makes possible the displacement of the double image of woman/nature. Nature is seen as virgin nymph or fertile and nurturing mother "in loving service of mankind," or as "a wild willful creature generating chaotic states that needs to be controlled," and, even worse, the bearer of "plagues, famines, and tempests."[17] Nature, identified with the female sex, was to be enslaved, inquisitioned, dissected, and exploited, an identification that justifies the search for power over nature and, over woman. Woman was seen as virgin if subjected to male desires, or as a witch if rebellious. Adored as a virgin, burned as a witch, who, symbol of the violence of nature, was believed to control storms, illness, and death. (The fact that "women also seemed closer to nature than men and imbued with a far greater sexual passion" became one of the major arguments in the witch trials of the sixteenth century.)[18]

After the scientific revolution of the sixteenth century the mechanistic view of the universe secured domination over the female attributes of nature. The virgin earth was subdued by the machine for the exploitation of the goods of the earth in a race where industrialization and technological progress, backed by an evermore rationalized view of the world, made the development of capitalism possible.[19] The process that privileged the mechanistic over the organic was also needed to control, dominate, and violate nature as female while excluding woman from socially and economically dominant ideology and practices. This approach to nature was based on a double system: one factual as it related to scientific laws; and one symbolic as machines transcended their own specific primary functions to give rise to a world of metaphoric and analogical relationships, ranging from the body to the entire universe.[20]

From a general opposition of nature/culture, other dichotomies more specific to architecture develop: nature/city and nature/architecture. Nature/city was already present at the conquest of the American wilderness and the concomitant development of the agrarian countryside, through the oppositional relationship between nature and machine. Throughout this process the mechanistic view of nature prevailed in consonance with the scientific revolution, and it continued to prevail on both sides of the Atlantic, certainly until Le Corbusier's Ville radieuse in 1922.

The locomotive, the machine that traversed the yet undeveloped land, generated another phenomenon: the appropriation and subdivision of land for towns and cities. The formal instrument that shaped this appropriation was Jefferson's one-mile grid which also became an urban footprint regardless of topographical conditions, transcending the opposition between country and city. Grids were drawn over the natural terrain as if on a blank piece of paper: cities without history. The grid as a spatially open-ended, nonhierarchical system of circulation networks anticipated what communications would produce later in a non-physical, spatial way. The gridding of America should be seen as the creation of the real modern city, an abstract Cartesian grid with no past traced on virgin land. A condition claimed in particular by Le Corbusier in his Plan Voisin of 1925 and a staple of early modernist urbanism more generally.

While modern cities were being built in America, modern examples of urban theory such as Le Corbusier's *Urbanisme*, Plan voisin, and *Ville radieuse* were being developed in Europe. It is in these early twentieth century projects that nature reappears as a major element in urban discourse. Ville Radieuse offers an excellent compendium of urbanistic ideology: "I go where order is coming out of endless dialogue between man and nature, out of the struggle for life, out of the enjoyment of leisure under the open sky, in the passing of the seasons, the song of the sea . . . The idea of the Radiant City was born over a period of years from observation of the laws of nature."[22]

It is worth looking into the apparent paradox in Le Corbusier's urbanism, where nature has an essential role in his critique of the conditions of the historical city, and in his development of an urbanism and an architecture whose avowed referent is the machine. To understand this "return of nature"

Plan of Chicago, Illinois 1834

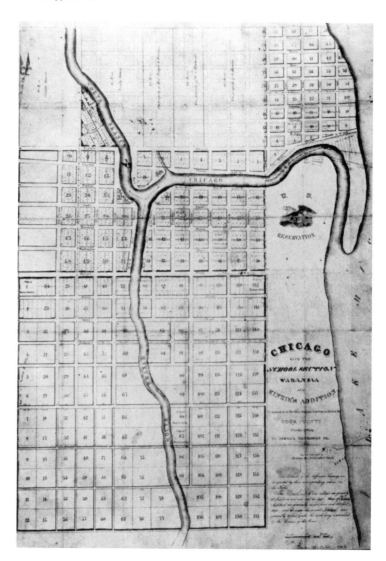

we must examine not only his writings but also his projects. Le Corbusier's critique of the historical city is based on establishing the opposition between historic city/nature, which could be translated formally into fabric/nature as stated in his critique of "the corridor street" in *Precisions*.[23] The green plane, a metonymic representation of nature, provides the formal background for the modernist notion of the city of object buildings as an alternative to the historical city of fabric. In the Ville Contemporaine, a paradigmatic example of modern urbanism, the American city's gridded nature is metaphorically (and unconsciously) transformed into an abstract gridded green plane dedicated to the movement of cars, while buildings (on pilotis) and pedestrians are lifted from the ground. Nature becomes an element in the machinery of circulation, or part of the modernist *visual field*. This field is not an organic entity but an artificial construct formally organized as an abstract horizontal plane where geometry imposes order and formal control. "In order to save himself from . . . chaos . . . man has projected the laws of nature into a system that is a manifestation of the human spirit itself: geometry."[24] While the incorporation of nature as an element of the modernist city was essential in generating the opposition between fabric and object, in its application this opposition becomes autonomous of nature, which, as if by a legerdemain, disappears. Nature is first suppressed, via a metaphorical maneuver representing it as a "green plane," as part of the urban machine; it is then relegated to a background, finally to be expelled by the economic-political forces of capitalism in a globalized market economy based on the exploitation and destruction of nature.

In modernist urbanism, where the city becomes the subject of architecture as a reaction to the historical city, the general opposition between nature/culture is transformed into the more specific opposition between nature/architecture. This new opposition is further articulated in the form of fabric/object, entering the architectural urban discourse as the historical city-of-fabric versus the modern city-of-objects on a green plane, thus generating a new morphology. In its subsequent application, however, what remains of this morphology is just the object, while the green plane, nature, which was the essential condition for the emergence of this opposition and morphology, curiously disappears. Nature then reappears in the discourse of modernist architecture and urbanism in a manner consistent with the mechanicism of the scientific ideology that is at its base, represented in the imagery of modernist urbanism as an artificial construct or as mechanized nature: In Ville radieuse sun, air and light, absent from the historical city, reappear managed and controlled by the machine (that is "exact air" and "artificial building site"). "To build houses, you must have sites. Are they natural sites? Not at all: they are immediately *artificialized*. This means that the natural ground is limited to but one function: withstand the strains, the weight of the structure (law of gravity). Once this is done we say 'goodbye' to the natural site, for it is the *enemy of man*. A home on the ground (beaten earth) is frightfully unhealthful; you no longer find it anywhere but in artificial sites."[25] The countryside is now "gay, clean, and alive," always placed in the context of the machine age. It is the artificial architectural order of modernism that regulates the relations between nature, city, and technology. The ideology of modernist architecture and urbanism is still based on the mechanistic scientific ideology, taking the form of *machinism*, an ideology that implicitly sanctions the repression/suppression of woman. Le Corbusier, wrote once more in *Radiant City*, this time on "Laws:"

The historic City and the Modern City,
Plan Voisin, Le Corbusier 1922

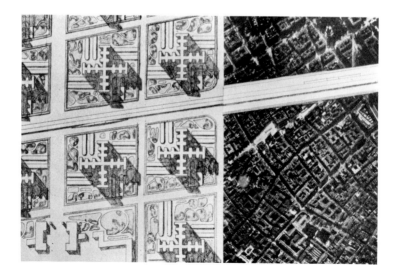

The laws of nature and the laws of men.

We live in the presence of three spheres:

Our dictator, the sun

The globe on which we live out our destinies: the earth

And a companion forever whirling around us: the moon

Woman, that power in conjunction with which we work, is ruled by this lunar month. We the men are ruled by the solar year.[26]

The urban realm thus discloses the historical role of the alignment of nature and gender, an identification that is once again key to the struggle for power and the engendering of power. The conception of the world as a machine in a fetishistic architecture that results from the application of the principles of modernist urbanism allows the double domination (or negation) of nature and woman.

Inscription of Nature: The China Basin Project

The city as object of desire is transformed into the city as the place where the forces of desire are set free. The China Basin project, much like Donna Haraway's cyborg, is "about transgressed boundaries, potent fusions and dangerous possibilities."[27] This project is a provocation. It is, to paraphrase Haraway, a fiction mapping our urban, social, and ideological reality, resolutely committed to partiality, irony, and perversity. It is antagonistic, utopian, and completely without innocence.[28] The project serves as a unique opportunity to examine some of the pressing questions concerning the place, role, and form of urban development and the position of nature in urbanistic discourse at this moment in time.

The China Basin is a three hundred acre site sloping down from the Embarcadero Freeway toward San Francisco Bay. The scheme assumes the creation of a new natural urban datum plane related to that of the existing freeway, which in turn is rendered obsolete and transformed into a residential structure. The freeway both defines one edge of the site and indicates the highest point above sea level. The China Basin Canal bounds the northwestern edge of the site and the San Francisco Bay lies to the east. An undulating blanket of nature covers the site and is punctuated by curvilinear public spaces varying in function and depth.

In the China Basin project, the smooth surface of nature replaces the striated fabric of the city, in the form of various street grids, which are buried under the site: a seamless continuity of activity flows under the smooth surface of nature, continuous flux without delimitation. This project addresses and encourages active production rather than the frantic consumption that characterizes most urban developments, a condition manifested in the proposed program. Zones of programmatic superimposition and interrelation radiating out of each "courtyard" are created, thus defining a *public place*. The boundaries determining various programs are left in suspense, undetermined, creating areas of programmatic instability, dissolving the barriers of institutionalized practice and reflecting the chance process of urban change over time. Intermediate levels provide most of the routes of movement. An intricate machine comprised of interlocking reels and platforms allows pedestrians to travel from one place to another in rotating, horizontal, vertical, and diagonal movement. At other levels, this is supplemented by more traditional communication routes. This project proposes to explore the possibilities of using geometries other than Euclidean, which is at the core of the Cartesian grids of both the American city and early twentieth-century urbanism.

China Basin, four layers: "nature datum plane," movement machine, public courtyards, street grids

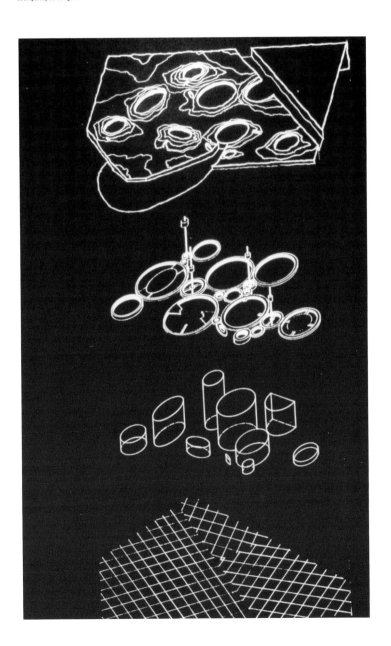

China Basin. Site plan

China Basin. Transportation level

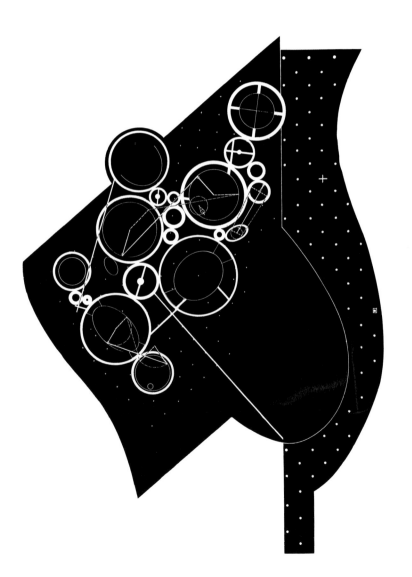

Programs

1. Amphitheater
2. Genetic Research Center:
Here, a place for the Genome Projects, the body as machine is scrutinized on the most scientific and analytic levels.
3. Museum of the Twentieth Century
4. Olympic Training Center:
The center is organized in linear fashion for swimming, running, jumping, skating, etc. The machines for exercising the body further elaborate the relationship between body and machine.
5. Radio Tower
6. Workshop:
The workshop is a center for production. Space is available for individual or group work in disciplines ranging from the fine arts and literature to cooking and computer animation. Spaces are oriented radially, with the most concrete physical activities—those requiring the most space—closest to the center. Moving outward, the space becomes more limited and the activities more abstract and conceptual. In section, each discipline occupies an L-shaped space. The individual spaces are stacked vertically while the horizontal space is maintained as a communal area for the exchange of ideas within each discipline. Acting as a two-way panoptic device, the workshops accommodate visual interaction between different disciplines.
7. Seat-in Screening:
The screening studio is a dual "seat-in"—a pedestrianised drive-in—open-air film theater with screens oriented back to back. The occupants are protected from the elements and audio-linkup is provided at each seat. The studio is intended to present sporting events and films not shown in the popular commercial cinema, including experimental films, documentaries, foreign films, and low-budget films.

8. Marketplace:
The marketplace is a mega-automat, where a structure rotates within a series of walkways. The structure itself is composed of four levels where the exchange of merchandise may occur. The consumer travels exclusively along the peripheral walkways, while the central structure rotates around its own axis, thereby making products accessible to the public. Adjacent to the marketplace are agricultural fields and workshops, where items are collected and produced for sale. Only those items produced on the China Basin site would be sold at the marketplace.
9. Aquarium and Oceanographic Research Center:
A semicircular wall with a diameter of 500 feet defines the entire site of the aquarium and oceanographic research center, which is composed of three major elements: a primary research tank connected to the China Basin Canal, an elevated aquarium tank, and, adjacent to the primary tank, a three-dimensional grid of pathways giving access to research floor space.
10. Baths:
The notion of dépense underlies the program, and here the pleasure of free bodies can express itself. The baths symbolize the intentions of the project as a whole: in this natural forum for discourse on the body, the public is encouraged to develop a new vision for the twenty-first century.
11. Baseball
12. Fields:
Here, agricultural experimentation takes place, generating products that may be obtained at the market.
13. Field of Solar Collectors

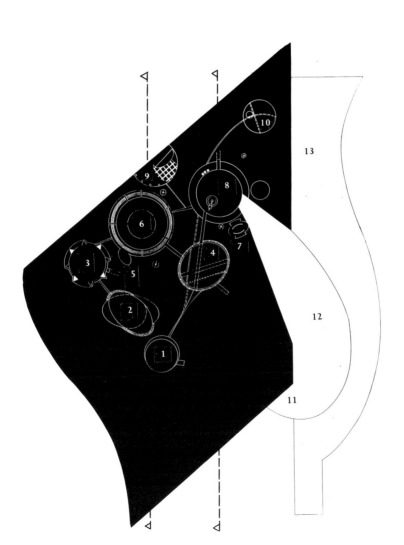

The city as object of desire is transformed into the city as the place where the forces of desire are set free.

Nature and machine join in the creation of collective territories. Residues of the forces that traverse the subject—the memories, the emotions, the rationalizations, the history, the stories, the assumed knowledge—are fixed by lines, by marks that project the forces of desire: "the survival of an experience."

In a movement that flows through earth and body, reaching through the gaze and into the depth of the universe, in the framing of infinitude, in the folding, collapsing of the sky onto the earth, through edges, borders, the borders of the body. Orifices and borders that are the makings of a body.

Border, edge, frame; the capturing and losing focus in an oscillating movement between the recognizable and the unknown.

Window, border, frame protecting the interiority of the subject from the collective outside while allowing the eye as shifter to bridge both worlds, as the mirror reflects the gaze back (to us). A seamless continuity of activity (of program) flows under the smooth surface of nature. A continuous flux without delimitation.

The Forces of Inscription

The natural machine, the point where nature, body, and the machine intersect, placing the subject and object on the same plane.

The traces of a body of woman which embodies desire, which is itself and the other.

Woman as gender constructing a new nature, it displaces the city to another place, which does not depend on the fetishistic object-building to achieve an urban pleasure.

Forces of Inscription, Diana Agrest,
Photomontage 1992

Notes

1. Sandra Harding, *The Science Question in Feminism* (Ithaca and London: Cornell University Press, 1990), 116.

2. See Jean Nicholas Louis Durand, *Precis des Lessons d'Architecture* (Paris, 1817).

3. English edition: Le Corbusier, *The City of Tomorrow* (London: John Rodker, 1929).

4. English edition: Le Corbusier, *Radiant City* (New York: The Orion Press, 1964).

5. See John W. Reps, *The Making of Urban America* (Princeton: Princeton University Press, 1965).

6. Barbara Novak, *Nature and Culture: American Landscape and Painting 1825–1875* (New York: Oxford University Press, 1980), 3.

7. Leo Marx, *The Machine in the Garden* (London: Oxford University Press, 1964) 4, 99.

8. Marx, *The Machine in the Garden*, 88.

9. Ibid., 15.

10. Ibid., 96; Novak, *Nature and Culture*, 5.

11. Novak, *Nature and Culture*, 4.

12. Ibid., 10.

13. Marx, *The Machine in the Garden*, 195, 206.

14. Ibid., 162, 165; also see Carolyn Merchant, *The Death of Nature* (San Francisco: Harper and Row, 1989) 194, 227–29

15. Merchant, *The Death of Nature*, 2–5, 20, 99, 214.

16. Ibid., 149–63.

17. Ibid., 2, 20, 127.

18. Ibid., 130–32.

19. Ibid., 2, 192.

20. Ibid., 192, 227.

21. See Le Corbusier, *Radiant City* and *The City of Tomorrow*.

22. Le Corbusier, *Radiant City*, 85.

23. See Le Corbusier, *Precisions*, (Paris: Editions Vincent Freal and Co., 1964). English edition: *Precisions on the Present State of Architecture and City Planning* (Cambridge: MIT Press, 1991).

24. Le Corbusier, *Radiant City*, 83.

25. Ibid., 55.

26. Ibid., 76.

27. Donna J. Haraway, "A Cyborg Manifesto," in *Simians, Cyborgs, and Women* (New York: Routledge, 1991), 154.

28. Ibid., 151.

A COLD VIEW

Margrét Harðardóttir

Any attempt to describe an attitude or approach to something as complex and ever-changing as architecture will inevitably be incomplete and outdated almost as soon as it is written. Explaining the search for what one intuitively knows to exist but has not yet captured is a delicate task. However, as it is a vital attribute of an architect not to avoid the uncomfortable, I feel compelled to write this text.

In writing one is forced to move outside the instant pattern of thinking, along the slow path of registration, which, like drawing, methodically attempts to transcribe thoughts in a coherent matrix legible to others. No matter what medium is used, the arduous task of analyzing, describing, and materializing visions or thoughts into a legible language is the same. Attempts to clarify complex matters often lead to simplification and consequently assume the format of a doctrine or manifesto. The problem is that once something is stated, it risks becoming "defined," closing it to further questioning. Consequently, it stagnates. However, there is equal danger of losing rigor and slipping into a euphoria of vagueness and fabricated reality, where freedom is confused with fantasy and sophistication with complication. True values are often the hardest to comprehend and portray, no matter what the language or medium.

A project's inception evolves around the exhaustive search for the threads from which the scheme will be woven. This search is without boundaries, and sometimes none of the source material can be used directly. The concept is often initiated in a trial of distinguishing between what matters and what is irrelevant. Some projects are simple in essence; others are based on more volatile ground. Each has its inherent characteristics and narrative, generated by its program and surrounding circumstances. Our role is to read the clues and create the conditions for the project to shoot roots and assume its independent life. We develop this condition until the project starts "talking back," until its identity is strong enough to influence further progress. The theoretical life of the project is integrated in the process, develops with it, and keeps maturing even after the building's "completion" and "possession": sometimes the concept only creates a condition, and nature or the building's users are left to continue its development.

The most difficult moments are perhaps entering a new territory that one has yet to learn to understand and operate. The development of each project is an ideal ground for clarifying thoughts and means of expression. For us, crude, multilayered explanatory sketches, reflecting disparate thoughts, become a tool for investigation and inform the mental vision of the project. Speed and change in the design discussion are essential to maintain both an intensity of debate and the critical distance to perceive the moment when the project fleetingly reveals itself from this turbulent field. Certain ideas or conventions carried on like bad spirits left over from an old project must be consciously exposed so that they can be exorcized from new work, allowing its real essence to be revealed. Concurrently accurate drawings backcheck and register the emerging scheme. This process continues through all stages of the design, which we scrutinize through a vital dialogue between the accurate and the ambiguous, the hard and the soft.

We have lately gravitated toward a base in Iceland, perhaps because we appreciate the optimism prevailing in a culture that is still growing and developing, where the categories male/female and native/foreigner and those of social class are less pronounced than in older cultures. Iceland does not have any deep-rooted historic architecture like the classical architecture haunting Europe; nor does it have an establishment responsible for shaping or teaching architecture. This forces Icelandic architecture students, who all travel abroad to study, to be more open-minded when learning the principles handed down to them by their host countries. It introduces them to a whole new language, perhaps more related to human proportions and social structures than are the climatic elements and masses in the landscape with which the Icelandic psyche is instinctively familiar. Perhaps this ignorance of a historic discipline gives a certain freedom and can in this sense be a creative strength; once something is known to exist, there is no driving need to discover it or even question it.

Our work was once introduced with the word *strange*. Perhaps this is an appropriate description, as the work results from instincts and conventions estranged from the European sensibility. Any cultural background makes its imprint; the question of what is strange intimately relates to the locale or origin— *étranger* in French means both "strange" and "foreign." Moving between cultures not only forces a reexamination of one's native culture but encourages a more critical approach in learning from others. It inevitably forces a continual reappraisal of established viewpoints.

On the other hand, living on an island encourages cultural isolation and a stronger bond with the immediate surroundings. Iceland's volatile, volcanic nature, both inspiring and potentially destructive, provokes a certain recklessness and intensity in the people whose very survival depends on geothermal energy and fishing. The continuous battle between the volcanic, shift-

City Hall Reykjavick, Iceland. 1988–1992. View from across the Tjörnin lake. The bulk of the south building follows an arc escaping the straight roofline, supported by slender columns rising out of the lake. The twist appears in the shadow falling over the south facade. Although the building is designed for a gloomy climate, it assumes a lively appearance during the sunny spells, when ripples reflect off the water onto the external skin and deep into the volumes within. (© Dennis Gilbert)

ing, tectonic ground and the ice-cold, windy climate makes the human presence here continually aware of its relative insignificance.

This has no doubt had its effect on our architectural vision and mood. The flow of nature cannot be ignored, nor can the mountainous masses and cavernous voids. The hallucinatory effect of distance and the fragility of proximity are always present in the back of our minds. This refers not only to phenomena such as mirage or the northern lights but also to the strange effect of various landscape elements combining into one plane on the horizon, despite the difference in their respective distances. Sometimes water, sky, mountains, and the fiery sun flow together into one image in which it is hard to identify or separate each element from the others or even to discern one's own position in the total picture. The landscape and the climatic elements are not read discretely but integrate with each other: a mountain is reflected in a lake as the sun breaks through dark clouds, while a veil of fog blurs the exact location of the shoreline, and the division of reflected and reflection.

Not only are the natural elements present in themselves, they leave traces behind. The windblown sand weaves its ripples into the snow. These natural patterns of repetition and their variations have preoccupied us and instigated our investigation of textures within and between materials and building elements.

The related transformation from natural to synthetic often recurs during the design process, as a foil to the omnipresent influence of nature. The synthetic often attracts us for its own sake, and we sometimes use it very obviously, declaring its artificiality. However, as all building materials are ultimately derived and processed from natural sources, they must be used at a level of refinement appropriate to the design. This is determined by their relationship to other materials, function, exposure, position within the composition, and required quality of aging. We try to get closer to the origin of materials and sometimes use them unprocessed so that they age gracefully and develop a more natural patina with time. This often lends a building a more convincing character as it ages—a central concern for us despite its current unfashionableness.

We are absorbed by the power of the elements and the particular degenerating and regenerating effect they have on buildings, perhaps because of our exposure to this severe climate. The sandblasting effect of strong winds and rain (often driven upward) has a self-evident effect on the detailing, junctions, and general feel of the building envelope. Snow and ice are as vital to the complete picture as the more obvious concerns of light and air.

Although there is no literal reference to landscape in our work, the Reykjavik City Hall, completed in 1992, is torn between its purpose as a civic organ and the physicality of its location. It sometimes appears as a sleek cliff by the lake, where birds can be seen soaring in the updraft. The building's shifting walls establish a parallax condition similar to the illusionary effects created when walking through the Icelandic wilderness. The same notion of layering is omnipresent in the fractured, volcanic ground. Thus, the penetration of light into the building, through deep north-facing clefts, is similar to the experience of climbing through fissures in a seismic landscape. The presence of nature is amplified by the surrounding water, which on a sunny day cloaks the concrete walls in a dazzling dance of reflected ripples. Conversely, in winter, steam rises from the lake, as gargoyles spill geothermal hot water into the lake, keeping it clear of ice for the bird life. (Steam clouds of this kind are a natural phenomena in other parts of the city and are in fact the origin of its name—"steam cove.")

These interpretations of nature in no way try to create an illusion of a natural environment but genuinely attempt to reflect laws of nature in the building. This does not negate human nature, which is a fundamental element of the total picture. Buildings are not only designed for and by human beings but are made by them. Architecture is clearly a product of the human mind, reflecting the capacity and character of the individuals involved. In this respect the source of inspiration always remains within the imagination.

However, some building elements of the City Hall, like the moss wall, are an integral part of the lake's banks and flora. Here the conditions were created and left for the elements to elaborate and expand upon, within a time cycle and process that belongs to other ordering systems. In winter the now established moss can be seen glowing behind a shell of ice, which continuously builds up and changes due to the relentless, soft trickle of water down the wall. In developing the surface finish of the precast concrete and lava moss-wall elements, we confronted how difficult those "other" ordering systems are to manipulate. No matter how we tried to achieve a relaxed distribution of the stone particles on the surface, it always reflected the ordered mind of the human being spreading them. Eventually we discovered that if the person throwing the stones was either angry or drunk, the distribution looked good.

This building was not conceived in a sunny climate. We developed the concrete to achieve the necessary color for the building to maintain freshness on a typical cold, wet, and windy day. Consequently, on those days the building appears most naturally balanced with the environment and in scale with the trembling ground on which it stands.

The City Hall is clearly affected by its function as a civic focus and a token of democracy. The fifteen columns of the south facade rise from the lake, representing the fifteen city council members who are entrusted with the delicate task of controlling the city. The council chamber is like a stage, offered to the street and a reflecting pool, so that passersby can observe the theater of debate. In this respect the building conveys our understanding of open democracy as something free-flowing and organic, which evolves within an understood framework of rules. The fascinating aspect is how this organism gradually develops and changes the network of rules, so that the apparently rigid lines readjust to another balance. This seems to be common to most good systems; the parallel with architecture is obvious.

The design of the City Hall creates a place for public debate and a forum for meetings and events rather than providing comfortable rooms for bureaucracy and formal receptions. During the building process critical voices talked of the lack of conventional symbols in a building of this type, such as a clock tower, long steps, and classical vocabulary. If our interpretation of the brief reflects a political move, it was to erase such clichéd symbols of power so inappropriate to the Icelandic culture. This country has never had the desire or need

City Hall. View from across the corner pond. City Council debates can be observed from the corner pond when passing by. The moss wall extends the length of the building as a primitive element anchoring it to the banks of the lake. The main entrance is through this green and wet north-facing wall. (© Dennis Gilbert)

to flex its muscles at anyone; its only struggle has been with the land and the elements. This is what we tried to capture and reflect in the spirit of the building.

On the other hand voices criticized the building for breaking the tradition of pitched-roofed, imported-timber houses surrounding it, referring to certain historic values and a responsibility to conform. In our minds, these made up only a part of a *genius loci* also described by the massive concrete bulks of the docks, the pond with its bird life, and eleven hundred years of culture.

The City Hall is not a vehicle for political messages but a reflection of facts concerning our existence. This is well presented in the two poems, selected by the mayor, etched into the windows terminating either end of the circulation axis through the building. The text to the east describes a morning in the wetlands surrounding the building, whereas the west sketches an evening scene. Although the mayor holds a highly political post in the city, the poems carry no political message as such but offer gentle observations about life and nature.

In 1989 we participated in a competition called Aktion Poliphile, for a private house in Wiesbaden, Germany. The brief consisted of a conventional list of space requirements and referred to the book *Hypnerotomachia Poliphile*, written by an Italian monk, Francesco Colonna, in the fifteenth century and re-

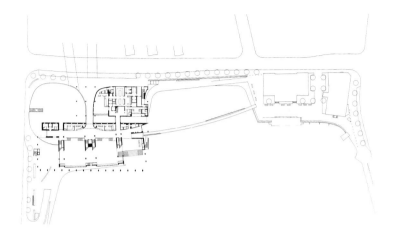

City Hall. Plan. The plan is shaped by long established pedestrian routes through the city, which extend the building via a bridge to the east side of the lake. The City Hall is incorporated into the banks of the lake, making it hard to discern where lake ends and building begins. Beneath the south building, at water level, is a forum for public gathering and socializing, whereas politics and public debate take place in the north building, more akin to the massive city fabric across the street.

cently the subject of much architectural attention. The concept of the house originated from a reading of the allegory, and in particular from Poliphile's struggle to overcome the darker sides of himself. The extremes of the human mind that Colonna describes are represented in the Wiesbaden house by the lighter, cooler, timber-clad "Delia" and the darker, massive, temperamental "Saturn." This scheme, created in Iceland without our having met the client, is necessarily free of any local influence from the site, which only existed as a diagram in our minds. However, the surrounding physical and social landscape later provided fresh clues for translating the original scheme into a building.

The choice of material was initially a tangential response to thoughts that surfaced during the construction of the City Hall but became more focused and precise as the idea slowly metamorphosed into a built reality. The creation of space is integral to the material. If anything this is the core of our approach: to give lines on paper a physicality at a very early stage and only then to allow the material and process to inform the space and theoretical life of the project and vice versa. Similarly, we are less interested in boundaries between inside and outside than in where the architecture begins or ends.

Material qualities are no less integral to the design of a temporary structure, such as the installation in Leeuwarden, Holland, where we collaborated with Icelandic artist Kristján Guðmundsson. The project offered the freedom

of working without site or program, resulting in a totally self-referential piece. The installation, built of light and sound, was a turning point in our perception of the material and the immaterial: light became an alluring element reacting to human presence, but sound acted as physical barrier forcing people away from the object.

This collaboration also allowed us to understand better how immediate our attitude had become and how we tend to evaluate things in relation to our own life span rather than, for instance, the life span of a building or a city. We have since gradually become more concerned with long-term effects rather than initial appeal.

The most obvious traces of the Leeuwarden installation appear in the starkness and massing of the Wiesbaden house and in the preoccupation with movement in relation to time manifested in the vertical wooden strips: The strips form a regular pattern on "Delia's" facades, which are manipulated depending on the balance of internal and external pressures affecting it. Sometimes the strips are a part of a solid wall; sometimes the wall disappears, creating a space caught between inside and outside; and sometimes the strip pattern disappears altogether, revealing large openings. In one part the strips lift off the wall to form a trellis. Nature has a grip on this trellis, through the roots of a vine entangled with it, pulling the fragile box back toward a larger organism. In "Saturn," nature plays a softer game of veiling the massive walls of the house in light, delicate creepers. Although these notions had existed in our repertoire for a while, they became more controlled and critical after encountering Kristján. The long morning shadow twisting across the east elevation as the sun rises is perhaps the clearest manifestation of the thoughts we developed through working with him, and reflections on the boundaries between what is seen and what is perceived.

The Icelandic High Court, a current project, is affected by similar notions, although the circumstances are very different. It is neither large nor complicated and seems a firm and solid block, though clearly pushed and punched about by the elements. The building's location and shape provide shelter from northerly winds blowing from the ocean over the site, but its vulnerability appears on the south facade, where its copper skin is lifted as if about to blow away.

City Hall. East facade, detail. The building's external walls are layered, holding passages and containing spaces. External and internal volumes are interdependent parts of the complete picture, as the spaces converse and interact. Large, robust elements reveal more refined and fragile parts on closer examination. (© Dennis Gilbert)

Aktion Poliphile — House at Wiesbaden, Germany. 1990 — 92. View from the north. The lighter "Delia" is poised on the extended arm of the more massive "Saturn." A small outdoor room is created between the two buildings, like a force field separating the two different parts, where one can look deep into the heart of either one. (© Norbert Miguletz)

House at Wiesbaden. View between the two buildings. "Delia" derives from the forest it confronts, but "Saturn" gives the impression of being the first building in the neighbourhood. The project is a play between the extremes of the environment, which parallel the poles of the human mind. (© Norbert Miguletz)

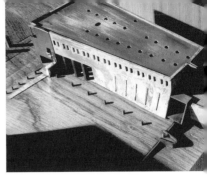

The building's external envelope is like an imprint of the internal and external spaces affecting it. Externally the materials reflect the nature of the city, surrounding mountains, and ocean. A rough-hewn basalt base connects the building with the ground and metamorphoses into the most prominent element of the envelope, a smooth basalt entrance tower. This relates to and reinforces links with the city center, a relationship further enhanced upon entering the building, where one is forced to turn back and view the city once more. The Icelandic rock *gabbró*, which contains delicate green crystals, is used as a touchstone between the massive basalt and the light, green-copper cladding, emphasizing particularly delicate places in the building, set like a precious stone.

High Court, Reykjavick, Iceland. 1994–96. Model. The earthbound part of the external envelope is of rough-hewn or sawn basalt rock, but the metamorphic rock *gabbró* is used for emphasis. The upper part of the building is clad in pre-patinated copper, in a sharp contrast with the surrounding state buildings. The south wall lifts up, allowing the grass lawn to continue under its fold up to the green roof area of the low block, flanking a new entrance square to the state offices on the north side.

Internally the materials used echo the ambience of various parts of the building. The same material can appear raw or refined, depending on whether it chooses to conceal its nature or generously expose it to the naked eye. Varying levels of refinement in the concrete finish betray reflections on the apparent baseness of crime and the relative sophistication of law. In places the concrete is left crude, whereas in others the fine consistency of a smooth-ground surface reveals shell particles among basalt, jasper, and opaline pebbles, which when mixed with concrete are normally left hidden. Public circulation is via a protracted, slowly ascending route of refined concrete floors beneath a crude concrete ceiling, setting a solemn, contemplative mood before entering the intensity of the courtroom. The entrance sequence further reflects our preoccupation with time and its irrelevance when under the spell of the Court.

The High Court is flanked by traditional buildings of national repute and therefore must tackle sensitive contextual issues. The project strengthens the existing street grid surrounding the site while creating external spaces of different characters, such as a small-town square to the northeast and a sheltered public garden to the south. Furthermore, the building establishes a clearly defined edge to the windblown hill between it and the ocean. As with so many public buildings, this project has been subjected to the winds of the political climate, which can be even more severe and unpredictable than their natural counterparts.

More recently we have been preoccupied by a theoretical exercise for a family house without site or location. The project has been developed in conjunction with artist/writer Forvaldur Fiorsteinsson, who has adopted the role of client. His sensibility and pragmatic outlook on life was concentrated into nineteen points that constituted essential ingredients for his house. The house is precisely defined by three lives, three personalities, and their relationships. It is organized around a daylit light well and has no view or connection to the outside apart from equipment for stargazing and meteorological observation, a gigantic multimedia TV, and shelves full of books.

The house is presented as a sequence of living: sitting, standing, moving, and resting. However the description is not complete, as the project continues its theoretical life through stories told by the client, describing events and conversations taking place in his home. In contrast to the Leeuwarden installation, which attempted to describe the ephemeral through a physical representation, the House of 19 displays real life via ambiguous means, attempting to portray how ephemeral existence fundamentally is.

No matter how much one loathes the fact, the building industry reflects the cultural state of the society in which we live. The crude realities that so often control the industry are an integral part of our existence. Building is an extremely sobering experience; just *how* to make something can completely change the original vision and requires flexibility in both thinking and opera-

House of 19. Imaginary site. 1994. Project. Model. The model represents the volume of the house as a series of planes. The project represents the dialogue between architect and client. It is realized in the space between the drawings and the client's stories.

tion. This is where theory is put to the test: ideas either become stronger or weaker when tried against a budget, regulations, and common sense. A critical client has a vital effect on a project and drives the architect's resourcefulness, often presenting a totally disarming viewpoint that nobody involved in architectural theory would ever dare to ask. Architects have perhaps been guilty of idealizing how people live, removing their field of expertise from the mundane world of curtains and domestic technology. In our experience, the architectural aesthetic grows out of all aspects of human existence, including the ordinary and mundane. Architects have been called the last alchemists for good reason, as no aspect of human existence should be outside of their scope; psychology and philosophy are as important as science and technology.

Architecture is about finding a way to represent the world in which we live. To achieve this we can only transfer our own emotions and attitudes to life into a physical form, no matter how dull, how irrational, how witty, and how instinctive; these are all essential. In our minds the question of aesthetics is a synthesis of a wide range of facts and emotions that must be crystallized first into a concept and then into a building. Sometimes a feeling offers the only accurate means of judging which catalysts are needed for an architectural reaction. If the result seems effortless and balanced, we feel a sense of achievement.

Aesthetics are often affiliated with the ideologies of beauty and perfection, closely connected to the unreal or unattainable, but we find that we are often left with the strongest emotion for the most crude aspects and failures of each completed project. Perhaps it is true that our very faults are our hopes.

Frontispiece: Jennifer's Shuttle, photo
by Rainer Hofmann.

Here is a picture: a sunny, late fall Saturday afternoon in a small, coal-mining town in Southwest Virginia. The town is nestled in a bowl of mountains, the Appalachian Mountains, their soft, tree-fuzzy mounds worn to an almost benign and benevolent presence. They are as old as time. Houses are perched here and there up the sides of the bowl, in a density that diminishes with altitude. We live way up, and our backyard rises at an angle sufficiently steep that a walk in it on all fours is the best way to go, especially if you are nine years old. This mountain is a heavy presence: immense, solid, protective, enclosing, comforting, eternal. It is so big and familiar that we often forget it is there; it is our ground. If you stand down in the bottom of the bowl on Main Street and look up, you will see vestiges of the postcard brilliance of an Appalachian fall. But the cold is coming on, and much of the crisp orange and red lies layered and soggy on the ground. You can see through the brushy covering of the mountain to the solid roundness of its form: ancient rock heaved up out of the earth, covered with the infinitude of life and death that is soil and humus and the things that grow and crawl about in it. You can also see, way up above our house, a wide sheet of barren grayness embedded in the side of the form. It is not the only one, but it is distinguished from the other outcroppings by its size and by a great slash of black, a stroke from a Zen painting, that traverses it: a small horizontal line drawn upon the great, brooding form.

It is, as I said, a Saturday afternoon. Fourth grade is a thing of the past and future, and Eddie Wayne Sexton (my heart be still) and I are bright dots on the mountain face. We are going exploring, going where no man has gone before, off on a great backyard adventure. Here, up close, the apparent solidity of the mountain's surface is transformed to a slippery, scratchy, redolent mix of dry upon wet, bright upon brown, warm upon cold. All fours is not a choice but a necessity. I am in front, inching up by scrambling to grab bits of branch or root. Eddie Wayne is behind, pushing me with warm, steady hands on my rear. I can do without his help, but my body, animal, entranced by the warm pressure of his, allows itself a little more weight, a little slide out of propriety into the pleasure of rot and gravity and heat. And now, here is the great rock outcropping above us; we scramble in earnest to reach the ledge. There, before us, its mute whisper barely perceptible, is the wonderfully horrifying fact that we are after: a great, black crevice in the mountain. The line is a crack. And though we are not sure of what exactly it is, we know that there is a lot of good stuff in there. Most of what is inside the crack is what the proper world of grownups would think of as undesirable: darkness, damp, snakes, bats, slime, feral mammals, bugs. But, for us, it is a treasure trove for imagination and invention. I have never forgotten it; I have never stopped being drawn to it.

Arakawa's spatter painting of the words, "A LINE IS A CRACK," suggests an opening up of the apparently smooth and seamless. A line opens up, like Robert Smithson's words.[1] The line as crack is an enormously compelling notion. As a metaphor, it presents the possibility that every inscription, every abstract delineation of human reality, every boundary, in fact, every kind of line drawn, is potentially a commodious space of exploration.[2] This is the space in which I work: inside lines that reveal themselves, upon close inspection, to be cracks full of hidden possibilities—caches of the undesirable and the marvelous. The thing to bear in mind here is the materiality, the three-dimensionality, summoned by the notion of "crack." A line is an appearance on or of something; a crack is *in* something.

In 1975, during my first week in architecture school, I was taken aside by the assistant dean to be given some advice. Here was the advice: "Young lady, if you have come to architecture school to look for a husband, I will tell you that you would have a much easier time of it if you would get a receptionist's job at one of the big firms in town. That way, you would meet plenty of young, single architects who might be interested in you. Architecture school is a long, hard road for a pretty, young girl like you." I didn't have the courage to tell him that I already had a husband, and thanked him for his interest in my well-being.

My work is the practice of a sapient primate who lives in a woman's body and who works with an awareness of that perspective. I am a woman who grew up in small towns in the South. I have fixed my hair, worn makeup, and worried about what I was going to wear every day of my life, including the days my children were born, since I was thirteen. I will flirt with men and share secrets with women until the day I die. I know what it means to be constructed as a thing and to be a container. I am convinced that this has to have an influence on the way that one sees things and containers, a taxonomy of objects into which architecture neatly fits, both in the sense of being a material mass with voids inside for holding people and furniture and in the sense of being a vessel of cultural and social signification.

Toni Morrison addresses both kinds of containers in a passage from her essay "Black Matters":

It is as if I had been looking at a fishbowl—the glide and flick of the golden scales, the green tip, the bolt of white careening back from the gills; the castles at the bottom, surrounded by pebbles and tiny, intricate fronds of green; the barely disturbed water, the flecks of water and food, the tranquil bubbles traveling to the surface—and suddenly I saw the bowl, the structure that transparently (and invisibly) permits the ordered life it contains to exist in the larger world.[3]

Morrison's powerful metaphor of invisible structures of control and containment aptly attends the work that I do. For, once you see the line that describes the bowl, it is impossible to look and not see it. This line is as interesting an architecture as the environment that is shaped and contained by it. And if we allow the metaphor to collapse *en abyme* for a moment, removing the fish from the bowl, and construct the bowl as a bounding condition of the "ordered life" of something called "architecture," the line of the bowl opens into ceaselessly ramifying and interconnecting tunnels, grottoes, and holes ripe for exploration.

It is the fishbowl kind of container, the unseen, obscure because it is always right there in plain sight and unceasingly familiar, that fascinates me. (The theme of Edgar Allan Poe's "The Purloined Letter" appears again and again in my work.) Perhaps because I have had occasion to bump up against that container in so many other aspects of my life, I have a strong sense of it; I imagine that I know it well. Yet when I *see* it, the ramifications and convoluted intricacies held within its plainness, its transparency, never fail to surprise me and reinvigorate my thinking about it.

I am contemplating a photograph made by the physician and photographer Hugh Diamond in the mid-nineteenth century. Although best known for his photographs of the mental patients in his charge, Diamond also made photographs such as this, a still life. Here is what I see: two large swaths of un-matched damask frame the picture right and left. They seem to be hung upon a wall that is a wood panel carved in ornamental relief; we see this surface behind and between the folds of fabric. Hanging on the panel are a lady's reticule and a powder horn from which hang what appear to be two ornamental tassels secured by round, polished horn connections. The reticule is large and sports a row of fringe across the bottom. Through the net we see that it is not empty, but its contents are indeterminable. Between the reticule and the powder horn is suspended the carcass of a rabbit, head down, ears crumpled against the floor of the scene. To the right of the rabbit sit three heavily ornamented porcelain and metal urns containing flowers that look to be primarily garden phlox, statice, and lisianthus. Before the urns sits a dark leather lady's shoe, toe directed as if it is headed out of the picture. The shoe has a sharply pointed toe and a three-inch heel in the form that I think of as Italian; its dimpled form tells us that it has been worn more than once or twice. In the lower center, just in front of the rabbit's head lie a dinner knife and a second object, perhaps a letter opener, whose lines form a diagonal connecting the heel of the shoe and the base of a classical vase against which the rabbit's dangling forepaws rest. Sitting upon the orifice of the vase is a great winter squash, whose stem points in the opposite direction from the toe of the shoe. To the left of the vase is a simple basket without handle. Most of the basket is taken up with an even larger dark squash, which crowds into overflow the basket's remaining contents: a leggy houseplant, a fat turnip, a bunch of radishes, and some dried leaves and husks draped back over and onto the vase and the floor. In front of the basket is a baby's metal rattle. Both the basket on the left and the third urn on the right sit on the tails of the damask drapes as they flow onto the floor, forming the framing corners, the container, of the picture.

The photograph depicts a captivating assemblage of small objects that I have just described in detail. What more can I say about it? I can point out its compositional geometry: a triangle, with the point of dependence of the reticule as it joins the rabbit's foot forming the apex, and the foreground row of objects delineating the base. I can tell you that this is a pleasing composition; the crowded assemblage of apparently disparate objects is satisfying to look upon. I can also note that it bears an uncanny resemblance to the foregrounds of certain paintings of centuries past: this photograph could almost be a detail from a fifteenth-century Flemish painting.

When domestic and profane objects appear in the foregrounds of such paintings, they serve as a kind of writing, communicating to the viewer the identities of human figures and deities in the paintings. This is a cryptic writ-

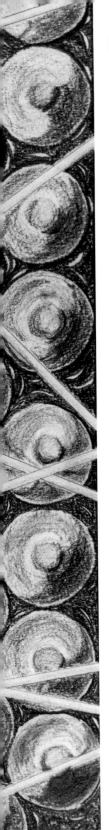

ing, a reification of rhetoric: the thing stands for something else. Collectively, they vibrate with allegorical potential, and to read them is to decode them.

In the still life paintings of the seventeenth century on, objects appear without obvious referents. They are sitting there, disengaged from any obvious iconographic vessels into which to pour their meaning. They are there, still as can be; but, as signifiers, they are both empty, simply there to look at, and very much on the slide.

The assemblage of objects that we see in the photograph, or in a still life painting, is a complex contrivance: a construction asking to be made from a pile of mundane objects. This construction goes beyond form and composition, although these are certainly present. This construction asking to be made from what is essentially a "pile of debris" deeply resonates with the construction of allegory that Walter Benjamin identifies as a historical construction intimately intertwined with a notion of petrified nature. ("In allegory the observer is confronted with the *facies hippocratica* of history as a petrified, primordial landscape."[4]) The ruin that Benjamin invokes ("Allegories are, in the realm of thoughts, what ruins are in the realm of things"[5]) is certainly a kind of *nature morte.* The reverse is true as well; the still life's ambiguous relation to time resonates with the melancholy of the ruin. I say ambiguous because the still life bears the promise of freezing, stopping, time; but both its presence as an artifact and its subject matter call out time's uncontrollable passage.

Indeed, a still life is like a historical construction: objects, "evidence," conjoined by something that is not there in the pile or in the picture: the structure of historical narrative. This is a structure of lines—sometimes a powerfully forced single line, sometimes a network of lines; and all of these lines are potentially cracks. In that the still life represents a cultural organization of material substance with significatory power, it bears a resemblance to architecture. The spaces among the objects constitute the core of its organization: its logic, its connections, its joints.

What is contained behind or within the lines of the still life? If we were to take an incising tool and make a careful slit in my photograph, then lift it and slide beneath, making of the line a crack, what would we find in this space? The territory of lines among the objects in the still life is like the smooth line of the fishbowl: it is hard to see, there in plain sight. But, again, once we see it, it is hard to leave it alone.

In my fifth year of architecture school, a major East Coast architect came to head a jury of student projects. He was, and is, an impressively astute critic, and I could hardly wait to hear what he would say about my project. Here is what he said: "That's a lovely blouse. Is it—? [Here he uttered an Italian name that I did not recognize.] The colors are magnificent on you."

I made my first performance construction in 1985, in collaboration with Robert Segrest. It was called the Project of the Undesirables and was performed at the Architecture Society of Atlanta. Its structuring premise was "A line is a crack." It wanted to be a virtual architecture "built" in the space of performance, which was the unceasingly noble, neoclassical Academy of Medicine designed by Phillip Shutze. It consisted of two people seated on wooden chairs on the stage facing each other, the space between us bisected by a line that traversed the space between a slide projector at the rear of the hall and the screen at the front. Crossing this line of light was our line of dialogue. The performance was organized by the four points in space that defined these lines and by four words: *map, mark, mask,* and *machine.* The images and the dialogue were structured geometrically and thematically to investigate the cracks in the lines and thus to invoke the presence of an architecture, the architecture that is always there behind the surfaces of lines.

My book *Architecture and the Text: The (S)crypts of Joyce and Piranesi* comprises a series of textual constructions, some meant to be performed, some simply to be read. The book explores the significatory powers of architecture and its allegorical potential, opening up the lines of several Piranesi etchings to reveal the possibility of complex virtual architectures in the cracks. It is informed by construction strategies that James Joyce used in making the text-world called *Finnegans Wake.* It thus suggests that the modern project of architecture is far from exhausted, but is not to be found in issues of style as we know it but in style as its etymology suggests—a writing, a cryptic writing, in which the proliferation of the allegorical (over the ordered and tidy symbolic) could be set in motion, reconnecting architecture to all kinds of physical and cultural matter.

The portmanteau word *scrypt* embraces the spatiality of writing, both inscription onto and incision into. The line is a crack; the crack is the possibility of architecture. The book sounds the resonance between the proliferation of meanings offered by texts of Joyce and Piranesi and the complexity of architec-

ture itself. The container that accords this possibility is architecture's old, symbolic role in culture.

Providing the theoretical bases for subsequent material projects, this work privileges the assemblage of material over the composition of lines and argues for the generative use of more complex and matter-friendly tropes than metaphor. It cuts into the smooth clean lines of the symbol to open it up to multiplicities of signification that are generative and regenerative and that create complex constructions connecting architecture to the world—the profane as well as the sacred, the mundane as well as the elite, the secret as well as the proclaimed.

The book is an assemblage of architectural texts, texts with virtual structures in them. The relation of these virtual structures to the texts is analogous to the relation of geometry (a virtual structure) to an architectural drawing. With these texts, I wanted to show something about architecture, to open up the lines into words and things, to show what is behind the lines, within the lines, to connect architecture to all the juicy stuff of the world and to demonstrate the nature of containers by making containers of text.

In 1981, during my last week in architecture school, I went to an Honors Banquet at which I received the American Institute of Architects' Henry Adams Medal and Certificate for being the top student in my class. I dressed for the day with great care, in a new, rather extravagant, pumpkin-colored blouse with great, puffy sleeves. I arrived in the hall at the same time as the second-place student, who was dressed in a starched white shirt and striped tie. As we approached our table, we were introduced by our dean to the local AIA president, who was to present the awards. The president leaned across the table and heartily shook the hand of my classmate, saying, "Young man, you've got a job any time you want it at my firm. Let's talk after lunch." He then turned to me and said, "My, that's a beautiful blouse you have on."

But making containers of text has its limits. Because there is a common understanding of words and sentences as simple vessels of meaning and not as material, I became increasingly aware that my work was not being understood by many beyond its outward appearance. "I loved your talk, but I don't understand what this has to do with architecture. . . ." "A very intriguing lecture, but why don't you show us some projects to illustrate what you are describing?" . . . "This is just a piece of writing. Why don't you show us your real work?" My response to this failure of understanding was born of a strange mixture of irritation (What thoughtless questions!), concern (I must work to bridge this gap of misunderstanding of what it means to work in architecture), and anxiety (maybe they have a point). I felt challenged to get beyond the judgment of conventional wisdom on the outward form of the work—writing—and explore similar spaces using materials that could be recognized as more clearly architectural.

I am entranced by matter, interested in stuff. Not only the petrified nature—wood, metal, stone, silicates—from which buildings are made but bark, bulbs, food, shells, ink, blossoms, soft metals, seeds, fur, fabrics, goop. And words. I have always loved the experience of the ink and the surface of the paper as much as what I am supposed to be focused on when I am drawing. I regularly instruct students who are drawing to draw with and on what makes their pleasure flow freely. Some of them know instantly and exactly what I am talking about; others cannot understand what difference the paper makes as long as it is the right color, isn't so bumpy as to make the pen jump, and is the right proportion to frame a particular composition of drawings.

Composition asks for quick recognition and naming: what is the name of this line? Once I can see and name the triangle underlying a composition of objects, or the circle in the square underlying a building plan, I am ready to move on to something else. Matter, however, is slow; it takes time to take it in. I can gaze into a hunk of obsidian for hours. The feeling is like being in love: I fall into it, into the pure fascination and pleasure of it. I can't take my eyes off its glowing depth. Obsidian is magic. The fact that it is made up of exactly the same stuff as granite fills me with delight. The same stuff, arranged differently, makes the difference between sensual magic and utter hard resistance. There is an important lesson here.

The project called Six Thousand Women, produced in 1988 with Durham Crout and Robert Segrest as an entry to the competition "L'Inventer '89" to commemorate the bicentenary of the French Revolution, materialized almost literally as a line that was a crack. A 1,000-meter slash was incised on axis in front of the Palace at Versailles, echoing the canal in the garden behind the palace. The site of the slit, one meter square in section, was the place where six thousand Parisian women gathered in 1789 to pressure the king to release food for their starving families under seige in the city. The slit, lined with

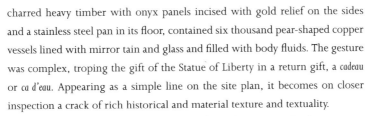

charred heavy timber with onyx panels incised with gold relief on the sides and a stainless steel pan in its floor, contained six thousand pear-shaped copper vessels lined with mirror tain and glass and filled with body fluids. The gesture was complex, troping the gift of the Statue of Liberty in a return gift, a *cadeau* or *ca d'eau.* Appearing as a simple line on the site plan, it becomes on closer inspection a crack of rich historical and material texture and textuality.

A fellowship at the Chicago Institute for Architecture and Urbanism provided the opportunity to orchestrate a more ambitious collaborative project. With Nina Hofer, Mikesch Mücke, Bob Heilmann, Jimmie Harrison, and several other students and colleagues, a constellation of objects, drawings, texts, and a large construction that collectively have come to be known as Tabbles of Bower were produced. Tabbles of Bower attempts to take the construction of *Scrypts*—the lessons of Joyce and Piranesi—into material possibility in the city of Chicago. The significance of Tabbles of Bower is not in the formal presence of the full-scale construction as the end of a line but in the spaces between, the connections among, it and all of its generative objects, texts, and drawings. This is its architecture.

The urban artifacts proposed in Tabbles of Bower are barnacle objects on the corners of Chicago buildings that provide possible accommodation for people who would otherwise be on the street to be out of the cold, wind, or rain. Not intended as architectural "solutions" to the problem of homelessness, they are signs pointing to a problem that is complex and extra-architectural. There is no way to know if there are human beings inside the barnacle constructions; whether people are present or absent, the constructions signify the conditions under which they exist. The oscillation of human absence and presence continually calls up the hidden human history of the city and is part of its power. We perceive this absence/presence, and it creates longing; it connects us. In the collective perception of this emptiness, we form some other kind of vessel.

One of the salient characteristics of the still life is the visual absence yet powerful presence of the human being. Recently I have begun to explore the possibilities of the still life as a generatrix of public architecture. The domesticity and the narrativity of the still life—the still life translated as little assemblages of objects that might be carefully arranged about our homes—is intimately connected to history (family history, personal stories of meaningful events, etc.). This relation of the domestic assemblage of objects to history and family culture suggests something to me about the city as the locus for something we might call urban still lifes. To place such arrangements, moved from the level of individual significance to that of collective significance, in the city is to move toward a domestication of urban space.

The vehicle that will advance this thinking is a constellation of objects called the Urban Still Lifes Project. It takes off from a certain reading of Dolores Hayden's idea of domesticating urban space and from Elizabeth Wilson's metaphor of the city as a shawl rather than some objectified "fabric." The project proposes arrangements of historical and allegorical constructions informed by the collections of objects (historical and otherwise) that people arrange about the spaces of their homes—"still lifes"—and by the African-American tradition in the South of marking graves with collections of domestic objects placed on top of the earth. These urban still lifes inscribe and remember the history of the city as it connects to its geography and demographics.

In a way, the urban still lifes return the still life to the medieval attribute. They inscribe the history (the attributes, the character) of the city in which they sit (still). Put another way, they serve as emblematic frontispiece to the city as text: they are concentrated collections of objects that contain the codes for reading the city as we traverse it. Sited in public space, often in spaces only seen from the automobile, they become even more powerful.

The still life elevates the quotidian and the mundane: fruit, flowers, fabric, domestic objects, tools, and spoils of the hunt. By so doing, it muddies the public/private dichotomy: here are all of these objects of the so-called private sphere set out for public display, and, furthermore, they are constituted as art, which is a cultural and civic domain. The everyday and the earthy are a large part of the lives of every single individual who makes up the thing called the public. Yet we constitute the space of the public as exclusive of these things. Public space is a proper, clean, anonymous space, unclaimed and uncluttered. Public space is not home. We are most uncomfortable with human beings who use "our" public spaces as homes, a fact that alone tells much about the division between public and private space—how the division divides us, cuts us off from each other, makes of "the public" an exclusive and strangely small club.

The still life provides a model for refusing to recognize a division between public space and domestic space, a division that always claims the inferi-

Detail, 18 *rue des Partants, Paris*
(*Urban Still-Life*), 1995. Drawing by
Jennifer Bloomer.

ority of the latter. It is a division that parallels that between high culture and low.

The Urban Still Lifes Project insists upon a complex and various public for whom the city is a home; it steadfastly refuses the strange propriety that always haunts the notion of public space. It insists that the city is a great, domestic space that houses the artifacts of urban culture and history in the same way that a family's home houses the family culture and history. It says, "Yes, the reticule and the powder horn and the squash and the dead rabbit belong side by side, and when we can see them side by side, there is something else here besides a collection of disparate objects." This "something else" is the fabric of Elizabeth Wilson's shawl, which is not a homogeneous "urban fabric" but a panoply of infinite variety, material, and color.

Here is what I did in my first job after architecture school: I ran prints, ran errands, and, finally, was promoted to a drafting table in the interiors department. Eventually, I was put on an architectural team. My first job there was to select sanitary napkin dispensers for the toilets of a shopping mall. I did that so well that in no time I had graduated to detailing the parking lot. I felt somehow successful, but guiltily so, because the other woman, a black woman from my class in architecture school, who had been hired there at the same time as I, was still running prints.

The glass that forms the fishbowl is not still. The line of the bowl is a crack of materiality that is moving, always moving, but so slowly that we cannot discern the movement. The material of the line, a mass of slowly cooling, molten silicates that appears to our eyes to be rigid and still, flows. That is what it is the nature of glass to do. Glass does not hold its line but rolls over and within itself, flowing, oozing, forming new spatial possibilities. This fact provides me enormous pleasure and a thin but solid, unassailable core of hope for our profession.

Notes

1. I refer here to a much-loved passage by Smithson: "The names of minerals and the minerals themselves do not differ from each other, because at the bottom of both the material and the print is the beginning of an abysmal number of fissures. Words and rocks contain a language that follows a syntax of splits and ruptures. Look at any word long enough and you will see it open into a series of faults, into a terrain of particles each containing its own void." Smithson, "A Sedimentation of Mind: Earth Projects," in *The Writings of Robert Smithson*, ed. Nancy Holt (New York: New York University Press, 1979), 87–88.

2. This seems a good time to acknowledge the constructive critiques of this paper by the extraordinary theorist of the line and much-valued colleague, Catherine Ingraham.

3. Toni Morrison, *Playing in the Dark: Whiteness and the Literary Imagination* (Cambridge: Harvard University Press, 1992), 17.

4. Walter Benjamin, *The Origin of German Tragic Drama* (1939), trans. John Osborne (London: Verso, 1977), 166.

5. Ibid., 78.

About the Authors

Diana Agrest is a principal of Agrest and Gandelsonas Architects, founded in 1980 and based in New York. She is adjunct professor of architecture at the Cooper Union and at Columbia University and has lectured and exhibited widely. Agrest serves on the editorial board of the *Yale Journal of Architecture and Feminism* and is author of *Architecture from Without: Theoretical Framings for a Critical Practice* (MIT Press, 1991) and *Agrest and Gandelsonas, Works* (Princeton Architectural Press, 1995).

Jennifer Bloomer is associate professor of architecture at Iowa State University and collaborates with Robert Segrest in a minor and supplemental practice. She has written and lectured extensively and serves on the editorial boards of *Assemblage* and *Architecture New York*. Bloomer is author of *Architecture and the Text: The S(c)rypts of Joyce and Piranesi* (Yale University Press, 1993).

Beatriz Colomina is a historian and theorist of architecture who teaches at Princeton University. She is the editor of *Architectureproduction* (Princeton Architectural Press, 1988) and *Sexuality and Space* (Princeton Architectural Press, 1992), which won the AIA International Book Award. Her latest book, *Privacy and Publicity: Modern Architecture as Mass Media* (MIT Press, 1994), has won the 1995 AIA International Book Award.

Elizabeth Diller is a member of the collaborative team Diller + Scofidio, a New York–based cross-disciplinary practice that incorporates architecture with the performing and visual arts. The firm's work, which has been exhibited extensively in the United States, Europe, and Japan, includes the books *Back to the Front: Tourisms of War* (FRAC Basse Normandie, 1994) and *Flesh* (Princeton Architectural Press, 1995). Diller is assistant professor of architecture at Princeton University.

Merrill Elam is a principal of Scogin Elam and Bray. Founded in 1984 and based in Atlanta, the practice has won many awards for its work and is regularly published in the international press. Elam is a corporate member of the American Institute of Architects and has taught and lectured widely in the United States.

Margrét Harðardottir is a principal of Studio Granda, founded in 1987 with Steve Christer and based in Reykjavik, Iceland.

Christine Hawley is a principal of Cook and Hawley, established with Peter Cook in 1976, an international practice based in London. A former chair of school at the University of East London, Hawley is now professor and director of architectural studies at the Bartlett School of Architecture at University College London.

Catherine Ingraham is an architectural theorist who has written and lectured extensively. Ingraham is an associate professor of architecture at Iowa State University and has been a visiting professor at Columbia and Harvard universities. She is an editor of *Assemblage* and author of the forthcoming book, *The Burdens of Linearity: Architectural Constructions.*

Françoise-Hélène Jourda is a principal of Jourda et Perraudin Partenaires Architectes, founded in 1980 with Gilles Perraudin and based in Lyon, France. The firm's work is frequently published in the international press and has been the subject of several monographs. Jourda has lectured and exhibited internationally on the work of the practice and has taught at l'Ecole d'Architecture of Lyon and Saint-Etienne, the Oslo School of Architecture, University of Minnesota, and the University of Central London.

Martine De Maeseneer lives and works with Dirk Van den Brande in Meise, outside Brussels. A former architectural editor of *Forum International*, she teaches at K U Leuven and at the Saint Luke Institute for Advanced Architectural Studies in Ghent, Belgium, and at the Academie of Van Bouwkunst in Tilburg, Holland.

Dagmar Richter has her own architectural studio in Los Angeles and Berlin, established in 1984. She is an associate professor at the University of California in Los Angeles and has taught at Harvard University, the Cooper Union, and SCI-ARC. Her work, including several international-competition winning schemes, has been widely published and exhibited. Richter lectures regularly on her work.

Nasrine Seraji-Bozorgzad runs her own practice, Atelier Seraji, in Paris and is a diploma unit master at the Architectural Association in London. She is visiting professor at Columbia University and Tulane School of Architecture. Her recent work has been widely published and exhibited.

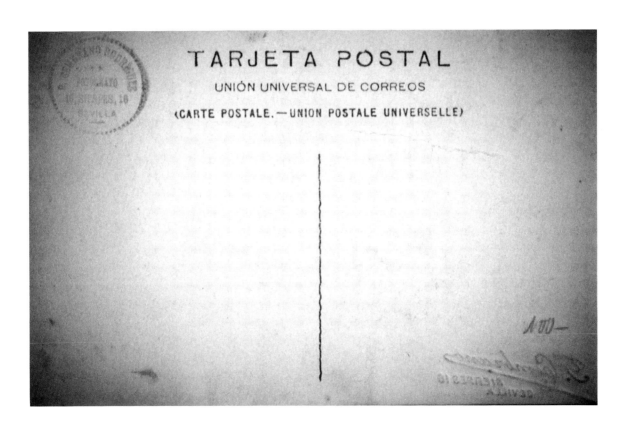

TARJETA POSTAL

UNIÓN UNIVERSAL DE CORREOS

(CARTE POSTALE. — UNION POSTALE UNIVERSELLE)